SOUPS & STEWS

Etc.

MEALS FOR LIFE™

FROM THE KITCHENS OF

HEALTHY CHOICE.

FOODS

CY DeCOSSE

INCORPORATED

A COWLES MAGAZINES COMPANY

CY DECOSSE INCORPORATED
A COWLES MAGAZINES COMPANY

Chairman/CEO: Bruce Barnet
Chairman Emeritus: Cy DeCosse
President/COO: Nino Tarantino
Executive V.P./Editor-in-Chief:
   William B. Jones

Printed on American paper by:
Quebecor Graphics (0196)
Copyright © 1996
Cy DeCosse Incorporated
5900 Green Oak Drive
Minnetonka, Minnesota 55343
1-800-328-3895
All rights reserved
Printed in U.S.A.

Library of Congress Cataloging-in-Publication Data

Soups & Stews etc.
p. cm. -- (Meals for life™)
Includes index.
ISBN 0-86573-985-4
1. Soups. 2. Stews. I. Cy DeCosse Incorporated. II. Series.
TX757.S6358 1996
641.8'13--dc20   95-48229

Table of Contents

*S*oups & Stews Etc. is full of soup, stew and chili recipes that are easy to prepare and full of good nutrition. While soups may need to simmer for a long time, their preparation time is short, and oftentimes, you can make an entire meal in one pot.

Etc. means that you will find additional recipes for the traditional accompaniments to soups: sandwiches and salads. These recipes can usually be prepared while your soup is simmering, resulting in a healthful, satisfying meal.

Menu suggestions appear with every recipe to aid in meal planning. These suggestions include the sandwich and salad recipes mentioned earlier, as well as simple complementary dishes. With hearty, full-meal soups, all that is usually needed to complete the meal are bread or crackers, and a light tossed salad.

Menu suggestions focus only on the main components of the meal. Beverages and dessert ideas are not included. Balance the menus with fresh fruit and low-fat milk, and choose low-fat desserts.

Soups & Stews

Soup is defined as a liquid food that can be served either hot or cold as a first course, main dish or dessert. Soups range in type from thin and clear to thick and creamy. They can be made from any combination of liquid and vegetables, meat, poultry, fish and sometimes fruit. Soups are generally simmered over a low heat to blend flavors and allow meats and vegetables to cook.

Stews are different from soups in that the pieces of food are larger and the liquid is often thickened slightly. Stews are generally cooked for a long time so meats become very tender and the liquid gradually thickens. Often thickeners are added to stews just before serving.

Equipment:
(1) 2 or 3-quart saucepan; **(2)** 8 or 12-quart stockpot; **(3)** ladle; **(4)** 4 or 6-quart Dutch oven; **(5)** long-handled wooden spoon

Stocks

Stock—also known as broth or bouillon—is a thin, clear liquid made when bones and scraps of meat, poultry or fish are simmered with vegetables and herbs. Stock is available canned, either ready-to-serve or concentrated, or in dried bouillon granules or cubes. These types of stocks are convenient but can be high in sodium.

Using stock as the liquid in soups creates a richer-tasting product than water. Since stock recipes usually make large quantities, freeze the extra. (Refrigerated stock will keep up to two weeks.)

Measured amounts of stock can be frozen flat in sealable plastic bags.

Fill ice cube trays with stock, and keep the frozen cubes in bags; two standard cubes equal about 1/4 cup stock.

Soup & Stew Tips

• The flavors of soups and stews blend and improve after a day of refrigeration.

• Individual servings can be reheated quickly in the microwave. Cover bowls with wax paper, and microwave on high until hot, stirring after every minute.

• To remove excess fat from soup, stock or canned broth, refrigerate it for several hours. Lift solidified fat off surface and discard.

• Once milk products have been stirred into cream soups, do not let the soup boil, or it may curdle.

• Thicken soup by puréeing some of the vegetables in it and then returning them to the soup. Other thickeners are instant potato flakes, a thin flour-and-water paste, a thin cornstarch-and-water paste, or puréed cooked potatoes or rice. Add each of these thickeners a little at a time, until desired consistency is reached.

• Garnish soups with finely chopped green onions, a dollop of sour cream or plain yogurt, snipped fresh herbs, toasted sliced almonds, popcorn, croutons or toasted baguette slices, or grated cheese.

• For a vegetarian soup, substitute vegetable stock for beef or chicken stock in a recipe.

• Stretch a thick stew or chili by serving it over hot cooked rice.

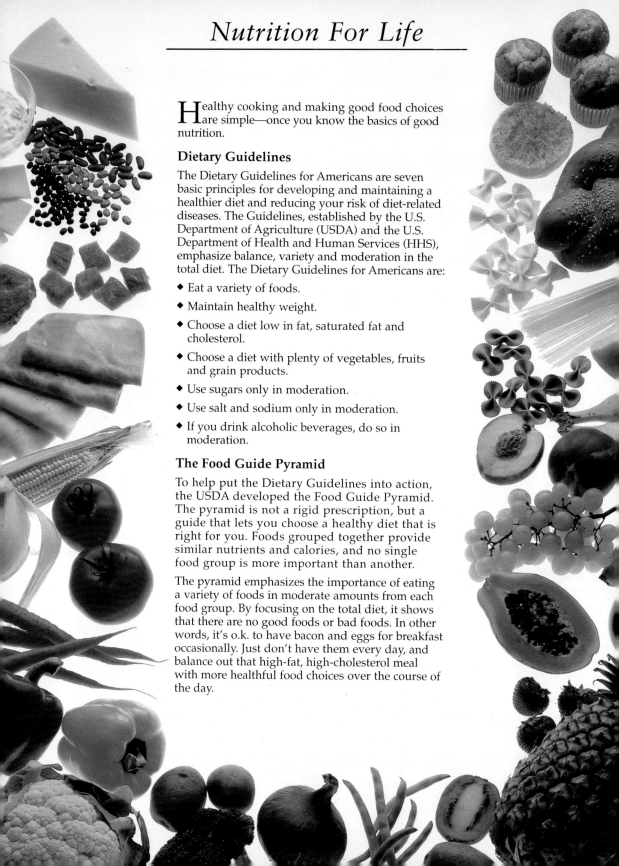

Nutrition For Life

Healthy cooking and making good food choices are simple—once you know the basics of good nutrition.

Dietary Guidelines

The Dietary Guidelines for Americans are seven basic principles for developing and maintaining a healthier diet and reducing your risk of diet-related diseases. The Guidelines, established by the U.S. Department of Agriculture (USDA) and the U.S. Department of Health and Human Services (HHS), emphasize balance, variety and moderation in the total diet. The Dietary Guidelines for Americans are:

- Eat a variety of foods.
- Maintain healthy weight.
- Choose a diet low in fat, saturated fat and cholesterol.
- Choose a diet with plenty of vegetables, fruits and grain products.
- Use sugars only in moderation.
- Use salt and sodium only in moderation.
- If you drink alcoholic beverages, do so in moderation.

The Food Guide Pyramid

To help put the Dietary Guidelines into action, the USDA developed the Food Guide Pyramid. The pyramid is not a rigid prescription, but a guide that lets you choose a healthy diet that is right for you. Foods grouped together provide similar nutrients and calories, and no single food group is more important than another.

The pyramid emphasizes the importance of eating a variety of foods in moderate amounts from each food group. By focusing on the total diet, it shows that there are no good foods or bad foods. In other words, it's o.k. to have bacon and eggs for breakfast occasionally. Just don't have them every day, and balance out that high-fat, high-cholesterol meal with more healthful food choices over the course of the day.

The Food Guide Pyramid

Fats, Oils & Sweets
Use sparingly

Milk, Yogurt & Cheese Group
2-3 Servings per day

Meat, Poultry, Fish, Dry Beans, Eggs & Nuts Group
2-3 Servings per day

Vegetable Group
3-5 Servings per day

Fruit Group
2-4 Servings per day

Bread, Cereal, Rice & Pasta Group
6-11 Servings per day

Reading the Pyramid

It's easy to follow the Food Guide Pyramid.

The bottom of the pyramid shows complex carbohydrates—the bread, cereal, rice and pasta group— at 6-11 servings a day. This group should be the foundation of a healthy diet.

The second level is made up of fruits and vegetables. We need to eat 3-5 servings of vegetables and 2-4 servings of fruit each day.

The third level is divided equally between milk, yogurt and cheese (2-3 servings a day) and meat, poultry, fish, beans, eggs and nuts (2-3 servings a day).

Most supermarkets now carry skim or low-fat milk and buttermilk; low-fat or nonfat yogurt, cottage cheese or ricotta cheese; and other low-fat cheeses.

A large variety of lean cuts of meat is also available in most stores. The leanest cuts of beef are the round, loin, sirloin and chuck arm. Pork tenderloin, center loin or lean ham, and all cuts of veal, except ground veal, are relatively lean. For lamb, the leanest cuts are the leg, loin and foreshanks. Chicken and turkey with the skin removed and most fish are lean meat choices.

The tip of the pyramid shows fats, oils and sweets. These include foods such as salad dressings, cream,

butter, margarine, sugars, soft drinks and candies. Use them sparingly.

Build a diet of good food choices based on complex carbohydrates, and limit your intake of high-fat foods. The recipes in this book make it easy to fit nutritious meals into a busy schedule. And you don't have to choose between good taste and good nutrition. You can have them both.

Balancing Your Diet

The number of servings per day that is right for you depends on the amount of calories you need to maintain your best weight. The USDA recommends the following calorie levels per day: 1600 calories for many sedentary women and some older adults; 2200 calories for most children, teenage girls, active women and many sedentary men; and 2800 calories for teenage boys, many active men and some very active women. Each person's body is different, however, and you may need more or less depending on your age, sex, size, activity level and medical condition.

For example, if your calorie intake level is in the lower range, choose the smaller number of servings in each food group. Or, if you are very active, choose the larger number of servings in each group.

Serving Sizes

What counts as a serving?

You may be surprised. Use this chart to determine how your food intake compares to servings on the pyramid.

For combination foods, use your best judgment in estimating which food groups they fall into. For example, a large serving of pasta with tomato sauce and cheese could count in the bread group, the vegetable group and the milk group.

Milk, Yogurt & Cheese Group

2 ounces processed cheese, preferably reduced fat

1 cup low-fat milk or yogurt

1½ ounces natural cheese, preferably reduced fat

Meat, Poultry & Fish Group

½ cup cooked dry beans, 1 egg or 2 tablespoons peanut butter count as 1 ounce lean meat

2-3 ounces cooked lean meat, poultry or fish

Vegetable Group

1 cup raw leafy vegetables

½ cup other vegetables, cooked or raw

¾ cup vegetable juice

Fruit Group

¾ cup fruit juice

½ cup chopped, cooked or canned fruit

1 medium apple, banana or orange

Bread, Cereal, Rice & Pasta Group

1 muffin, dinner roll or slice bread

1 ounce ready-to-eat cereal

½ cup cooked cereal, rice or pasta

2 Add juice, wine, sugar, salt, marjoram and pepper to skillet. Cover. Reduce heat to low. Let simmer for 12 to 15 minutes, or until meat near bone is no longer pink and juices run clear.

3 Remove chicken from skillet and place on serving platter. Cover to keep warm. Set aside. Using whisk, stir cornstarch mixture into skillet. Add grapes and peel. Cook for 1½ to 2½ minutes, or until sauce is thickened and translucent, stirring constantly. Spoon over chicken.

Nutrition Facts	Amount/serving	%DV*	Amount/serving	%DV*
Serving Size 1 breast half (136g)	Total Fat 5g	7%	Total Carbohydrate 9g	3%
	Saturated Fat 1g	5%	Dietary Fiber <1g	1%
Servings per Recipe 6	Cholesterol 55mg	18%	Sugars 8g	
Calories 164 Calories from Fat 41	Sodium 135mg	6%	Protein 21g	
	Vitamin A 0% • Vitamin C 20% • Calcium 2% • Iron 4%			
	*Percent Daily Values (DV) are based on a 2000 calorie diet			

Menu Planning Guide

One serving of this recipe provides:
 1 Meat, Poultry & Fish
 ½ Fruit

Diet Exchanges:
3 lean meat • ½ fruit

Nutritional Information

Each recipe in this book is followed by a Nutrition Facts chart and diet exchanges. The Nutrition Facts chart is similar to those that appear on food product labels. The diet exchange system is used by people with diabetes and persons on a weight-control diet, to estimate the calories, protein, carbohydrate and fat content of a food or meal. Diet exchanges are based on exchange lists and are not the same as pyramid servings.

Nutrition Facts state serving size, servings per container and the amount of calories, calories from fat and other nutrients per serving. Percentage of Daily Value gives you an idea of what percentage of the day's nutrients comes from the recipe. The percentages of the Daily Value of fat, saturated fat, cholesterol, sodium, total carbohydrate and dietary fiber are based on a 2,000-calorie-per-day diet. (Daily values will vary from person to person depending on calorie needs.) The Dietary Guidelines recommend that no more than 30% of your calories come from fat. So, if you are eating 2,000 calories per day, your total fat intake should be less than 65 grams.

If alternate ingredients are given in the recipe's ingredient list, such as a choice between cholesterol-free egg product and egg, the nutritional analysis applies to the first ingredient listed. Optional ingredients are not included in the analysis. For pasta and rice, the nutritional information applies to the plain, boiled item without salt or fat added.

Recipe serving sizes are based on federal reference numbers for serving sizes.

The Pyramid in This Book

Each recipe in this book includes a Menu Planning Guide that shows the number of servings from each pyramid group that one serving of that recipe provides. A daily total of these "pyramid servings" shows how your diet compares to the USDA recommendations.

When the tip of the pyramid has a dot, the item may contain added fat or fat beyond the natural fat content of lean or low-fat items in the food groups. Refer to the Nutrition Facts chart to check the total amount of fat per serving. A tip with a dot may also indicate that the recipe contains added sugar. Refer to the recipe to determine the number of teaspoons of sugar you will eat.

The number of servings is rounded to the nearest half. If no figures appear next to or within the pyramid, it means that serving sizes are negligible.

If the tip of the pyramid has no dot, a serving contains less than 3 grams added fat or less than 1 teaspoon added sugar.

Beef Stock

2 lbs. well-trimmed beef soup bones with meat
1 tablespoon vegetable oil
2 medium carrots, cut into 1-inch pieces (1 cup)
2 stalks celery, cut into 1-inch pieces (1 cup)
1 medium onion, cut into 1-inch chunks (1 cup)
1 tablespoon margarine or butter
1 cup boiling water
14 cups cold water
1 tablespoon no-salt-added tomato paste
2 whole cloves garlic, peeled
2 sprigs fresh parsley
1 sprig fresh thyme
1 bay leaf

8 cups

1 Heat oven to 375°F. Cut most meat from bones. Cut meat into 1-inch chunks. Place meat and bones in 13 x 9-inch baking pan. Drizzle oil evenly over meat and bones, stirring to coat. Bake for 45 to 50 minutes, or until meat is well browned, but not burned, stirring occasionally. Drain and discard fat from pan.

2 Meanwhile, combine carrots, celery, onion and margarine in 8-quart stockpot. Cook over medium heat for 12 to 16 minutes, or until vegetables are tender-crisp and onions are light golden brown, stirring occasionally.

3 Transfer browned meat and bones from baking pan to stockpot. Pour boiling water into pan, scraping bottom to loosen browned bits. Pour mixture into stockpot. Add remaining ingredients to stockpot. Bring to simmer, skimming surface of stock frequently.

4 Reduce heat to medium-low. Simmer, partially covered, for 4 hours, skimming occasionally and adding additional hot water as needed to keep meat and vegetables covered. Strain and discard solids from stock. Add enough additional water to stock to equal 8 cups. Cool. Cover. Chill overnight.

5 Skim fat off surface of stock. Freeze any stock not immediately used, in pre-measured amounts, in small plastic food-storage bags or containers.

Tip: If using plastic food-storage bags, freeze bags flat so they will be easier to store in the freezer. Label all bags with the type of stock, amount, and the date the stock was made.

Nutrition Facts	Amount/serving	%DV*	Amount/serving	%DV*	Menu Planning Guide
Serving Size 1 cup (256g)	Total Fat 0g	0%	Total Carbohydrate 2g	1%	One serving of this recipe provides:
Servings per Recipe 8	Saturated Fat 0g	0%	Dietary Fiber 0g	0%	
Calories 24	Cholesterol 0mg	0%	Sugars 0g		
Calories from Fat 0	Sodium 10mg	0%	Protein 1g		
	Vitamin A 2% • Vitamin C 2% • Calcium 0% • Iron 0%				Diet Exchanges:
	*Percent Daily Values (DV) are based on a 2000 calorie diet.				free

Chicken Stock†

- 2 lbs. chicken wings*, skin on
- 1 medium carrot, cut into ½-inch pieces (½ cup)
- 1 stalk celery, cut into ½-inch pieces (½ cup)
- 1 small onion, cut into ½-inch chunks (½ cup)
- 1 tablespoon margarine or butter
- 10 cups cold water
- 2 whole cloves garlic, peeled
- 2 sprigs fresh parsley
- 1 sprig fresh thyme
- 1 bay leaf

8 cups

Assorted raw or cooked chicken bones and scraps may be used instead.

1 Cut each chicken wing into 3 pieces. Set aside. In 8-quart stockpot, combine carrot, celery, onion and margarine. Cook over medium heat for 10 to 12 minutes, or until vegetables are tender-crisp and onions are light golden brown, stirring occasionally. Stir in wings and remaining ingredients. Bring to simmer, skimming surface of stock frequently.

2 Reduce heat to medium-low. Simmer, partially covered, for 1½ hours, skimming occasionally and adding additional hot water as needed to keep wings and vegetables covered. Strain and discard solids from stock. Add enough additional water to stock to equal 8 cups. Cool. Cover. Chill overnight.

3 Skim fat off surface of stock. Freeze any stock not immediately used, in pre-measured amounts, in small plastic food-storage bags or containers.

Vegetable Stock

- 4 medium carrots, cut into 2-inch pieces (2 cups)
- 2 medium onions, cut into 2-inch chunks (2 cups)
- 2 stalks celery, cut into 2-inch pieces (1 cup)
- 1 small leek, cut into 2-inch lengths (1 cup)
- 2 tablespoons margarine or butter
- 10 cups cold water
- 2 whole cloves garlic, peeled
- 2 sprigs fresh parsley
- 1 sprig fresh thyme
- 1 dried shiitake mushroom (optional)
- 1 bay leaf
- 6 whole black peppercorns

8 cups

1 Combine carrots, onions, celery, leek and margarine in 8-quart stockpot. Cook over medium heat for 18 to 20 minutes, or until vegetables are tender-crisp and onions are light golden brown, stirring occasionally. Add remaining ingredients. Bring to simmer, skimming surface of stock frequently.

2 Reduce heat to medium-low. Simmer, partially covered, for 1½ hours, skimming occasionally and adding additional hot water as needed to keep vegetables covered. Strain and discard solids from stock. Add enough additional water to stock to equal 8 cups. Cool. Cover. Chill overnight.

3 Skim fat off surface of stock. Freeze any stock not immediately used, in pre-measured amounts, in small plastic food-storage bags or containers.

†Nutrition Facts	Amount/serving	%DV*	Amount/serving	%DV*
Serving Size 1 cup (256g) Servings per Recipe 8 Calories 23 Calories from Fat 0	Total Fat 0g	0%	Total Carbohydrate 2g	1%
	Saturated Fat 0g	0%	Dietary Fiber 0g	0%
	Cholesterol 0mg	0%	Sugars 0g	
	Sodium 5mg	0%	Protein 1g	
	Vitamin A 0% • Vitamin C 0% • Calcium 0% • Iron 0%			
	*Percent Daily Values (DV) are based on a 2000 calorie diet.			

Menu Planning Guide

One serving of this recipe provides:

Diet Exchanges:

free

Meatball Carbonade

Serve with a whole wheat dinner roll and a tossed salad

½ lb. lean ground beef, crumbled

½ teaspoon instant minced garlic

1 can (14½ oz.) ready-to-serve beef broth

¼ cup all-purpose flour

2 tablespoons tomato paste

¼ teaspoon dried thyme leaves

¼ teaspoon pepper

1 medium onion, sliced and separated into rings

2 medium carrots, cut diagonally into thin
    slices (1 cup)

1 teaspoon vegetable oil

1 medium russet potato, peeled and cut into
    ⅛-inch slices (2 cups)

1 can (12 oz.) beer

1 bay leaf

2 tablespoons snipped fresh parsley

6 servings

1 Combine ground beef and garlic in small mixing bowl. Shape into 16 meatballs, about 1 inch in diameter. Set aside. In 4-cup measure, combine broth, flour, tomato paste, thyme and pepper. Stir with whisk until smooth. Set aside.

2 Combine onion, carrots and oil in 12-inch nonstick skillet. Cook over medium heat for 5 to 7 minutes, or until vegetables are tender-crisp, stirring frequently. Stir in broth mixture, potato, beer and bay leaf. Bring to boil. Reduce heat to low. Simmer for 17 to 19 minutes, or until potato is tender, stirring occasionally.

3 Add meatballs and parsley. Increase heat to medium. Cook for 7 to 9 minutes, or until meatballs are firm and no longer pink, stirring occasionally. Remove and discard bay leaf before serving.

Nutrition Facts	Amount/serving	%DV*	Amount/serving	%DV*
Serving Size 1 cup (265g)	Total Fat 3g	4%	Total Carbohydrate 21g	7%
Servings per Recipe 6	Saturated Fat 1g	3%	Dietary Fiber 2g	10%
Calories 157	Cholesterol 20mg	7%	Sugars 3g	
Calories from Fat 23	Sodium 376mg	16%	Protein 10g	

Vitamin A 110% • Vitamin C 15% • Calcium 2% • Iron 10%

*Percent Daily Values (DV) are based on a 2000 calorie diet.

Menu Planning Guide

One serving of this recipe provides:

½ Meat, Poultry & Fish
1 Vegetable

Diet Exchanges:

1 lean meat • 1 starch • ½ vegetable

Irish Stew

Serve with cooked cabbage or mixed cabbage salad

1-lb. well-trimmed boneless lamb leg,
   cut into 1-inch cubes

2 cups cubed peeled red potatoes
   (3/4-inch cubes)

8 oz. whole fresh baby carrots

2 small onions, sliced

1½ teaspoons instant beef bouillon granules

1 teaspoon dried oregano leaves

½ teaspoon dried basil leaves

½ teaspoon pepper

¼ teaspoon dried summer savory

2½ cups boiling water

4 servings

1 Combine all ingredients, except water, in 4-quart saucepan. Pour water over mixture. Bring to boil over high heat. Cover. Reduce heat to low. Simmer for 1½ to 2 hours, or until meat and vegetables are tender and liquid is almost completely absorbed.

Nutrition Facts	Amount/serving	%DV*	Amount/serving	%DV*
Serving Size approximately 1 cup (396g)	Total Fat 7g	11%	Total Carbohydrate 25g	8%
	Saturated Fat 2g	12%	Dietary Fiber 4g	15%
Servings per Recipe 4	Cholesterol 76mg	25%	Sugars 5g	
Calories 271	Sodium 451mg	19%	Protein 27g	
Calories from Fat 64	Vitamin A 260% • Vitamin C 15% • Calcium 6% • Iron 15%			
	*Percent Daily Values (DV) are based on a 2000 calorie diet.			

Menu Planning Guide

One serving of this recipe provides:

1 Meat, Poultry & Fish
2 Vegetable

Diet Exchanges:

3 lean meat • 1 starch • 1 vegetable

Lamb Stew

Serve with fresh Italian bread and a tossed green salad

2 tablespoons all-purpose flour

1 to 2 tablespoons chili powder, divided

2 teaspoons paprika

1 - lb. well-trimmed boneless lamb leg, cut into
 ³⁄₄-inch cubes

1 small onion, chopped (¹⁄₂ cup)

1 clove garlic, minced

3¹⁄₂ cups water

1 can (14¹⁄₂ oz.) diced tomatoes, undrained

1 cup cubed peeled potato (¹⁄₂-inch cubes)

1 medium carrot, chopped (¹⁄₂ cup)

1 stalk celery, sliced (¹⁄₂ cup)

1 tablespoon tomato paste

¹⁄₂ teaspoon salt

¹⁄₄ teaspoon cayenne

1 cup coarsely torn fresh mushrooms

¹⁄₂ cup frozen peas

¹⁄₂ cup frozen cut green beans

8 servings

1 Combine flour, 1 teaspoon chili powder and the paprika in large plastic food-storage bag. Add lamb cubes. Seal bag. Shake to coat. Set aside.

2 Spray 4-quart saucepan with nonstick vegetable cooking spray. Heat saucepan over medium-high heat. Add lamb, onion and garlic. Cook for 8 to 10 minutes, or until meat is no longer pink, stirring frequently. Stir in remaining chili powder, the water, tomatoes, potato, carrot, celery, tomato paste, salt and cayenne.

3 Bring to boil. Reduce heat to low. Cover. Simmer for 45 minutes. Uncover. Simmer for additional 45 minutes to 1 hour 15 minutes, or until meat is tender, stirring in mushrooms, peas and beans during last 15 minutes.

Nutrition Facts	Amount/serving	%DV*	Amount/serving	%DV*
Serving Size 1 cup (290g) Servings per Recipe 8 Calories 166 Calories from Fat 46	Total Fat 5g	8%	Total Carbohydrate 14g	5%
	Saturated Fat 2g	9%	Dietary Fiber 3g	11%
	Cholesterol 46mg	15%	Sugars 4g	
	Sodium 306mg	13%	Protein 17g	

Vitamin A 70% • Vitamin C 25% • Calcium 4% • Iron 15%
*Percent Daily Values (DV) are based on a 2000 calorie diet.

Menu Planning Guide

One serving of this recipe provides:
 1 Meat, Poultry & Fish
1¹⁄₂ Vegetable

Diet Exchanges:

2 lean meat • ¹⁄₂ starch • 1 vegetable

Pork Burgoo

Serve with corn bread and fruit salad

1½ lbs. well-trimmed pork tenderloin, cut into
　　¾-inch cubes

¾ cup chopped green pepper

1 small onion, chopped (½ cup)

1 stalk celery, sliced (½ cup)

1 medium carrot, sliced (½ cup)

2 cups water

1 can (14½ oz.) whole tomatoes, undrained
　　and cut up

1 cup cubed red potato (½-inch cubes)

1 cup shredded green cabbage

½ cup frozen cut okra

½ cup frozen lima beans

½ cup frozen corn

2 tablespoons tomato paste

2 tablespoons snipped fresh parsley

½ teaspoon salt

¼ teaspoon pepper

6 servings

Note: Burgoo, a thick stew full of meats and a wide variety of vegetables, is popular at large gatherings in the South.

1 Spray 6-quart stockpot with nonstick vegetable cooking spray. Heat stockpot over medium-high heat. Add pork, green pepper, onion, celery and carrot. Cook for 8 to 10 minutes, or until meat is no longer pink and vegetables are tender, stirring occasionally. Drain.

2 Stir in remaining ingredients. Bring to boil over high heat. Reduce heat to medium-low. Simmer for 30 to 45 minutes, or until meat is very tender and stew is thickened, stirring occasionally.

Nutrition Facts	Amount/serving	%DV*	Amount/serving	%DV*
Serving Size approximately 1 cup (427g)	Total Fat 6g	10%	Total Carbohydrate 21g	7%
	Saturated Fat 2g	10%	Dietary Fiber 5g	18%
Servings per Recipe 6	Cholesterol 84mg	28%	Sugars 6g	
Calories 263 Calories from Fat 56	Sodium 423mg	18%	Protein 31g	
	Vitamin A 80% • Vitamin C 60% • Calcium 6% • Iron 15%			
	*Percent Daily Values (DV) are based on a 2000 calorie diet.			

Menu Planning Guide
One serving of this recipe provides:
　1 Meat, Poultry & Fish
　2½ Vegetable

Diet Exchanges:
3 lean meat • ½ starch • 2 vegetable

Hearty Minestrone Soup

Serve with Caesar salad and Italian bread

1/3 cup pesto, divided

1/2 lb. beef stew meat, cut into 1/2-inch pieces

2 medium carrots, sliced (1 cup)

2 stalks celery, chopped (1 cup)

1 medium onion, chopped (1 cup)

4 oz. fresh green beans, cut into 2-inch
   lengths (1 cup)

8 cups water

1/4 cup dehydrated vegetable flakes

1 tablespoon instant chicken bouillon granules

1 can (28 oz.) whole tomatoes, drained and
   cut up

1 can (16 oz.) red kidney beans, rinsed and
   drained

1 1/2 cups uncooked rainbow rotini

1 cup uncooked bow-tie pasta

1 medium zucchini, sliced (1 cup)

1/2 cup uncooked macaroni rings

12 servings

1 Heat 1 tablespoon pesto over medium-high heat in 6-quart Dutch oven or stock-pot. Add stew meat. Cook for 4 to 5 minutes, or until meat is browned, stirring frequently. Add carrots, celery, onion and beans. Cook for 3 to 5 minutes, or until onions are tender, stirring frequently.

2 Add water, remaining pesto, the vegetable flakes and bouillon. Bring mixture to boil over medium heat, stirring frequently. Reduce heat to low. Simmer, partially covered, for 45 minutes to 1 hour, or until meat is tender, stirring occasionally.

3 Return mixture to boil over medium heat. Add remaining ingredients. Reduce heat to low. Simmer for 15 to 20 minutes, or until pasta is tender and soup is hot, stirring occasionally.

Nutrition Facts	Amount/serving	%DV*	Amount/serving	%DV*
Serving Size 1 cup (374g)	Total Fat 7g	10%	Total Carbohydrate 28g	9%
Servings per Recipe 12	Saturated Fat 2g	10%	Dietary Fiber 5g	20%
Calories 213	Cholesterol 17mg	5%	Sugars 6g	
Calories from Fat 61	Sodium 502mg	21%	Protein 11g	

Vitamin A 40% • Vitamin C 25% • Calcium 10% • Iron 15%
*Percent Daily Values (DV) are based on a 2000 calorie diet.

Menu Planning Guide

One serving of this recipe provides:

1/2 Meat, Poultry & Fish
 1 Vegetable
1/2 Bread, Cereal, Rice & Pasta

Diet Exchanges:

• 1/2 medium-fat meat • 1 1/2 starch • 1 vegetable

Chicken Gumbo

Serve with hot cooked white rice

1/4 cup all-purpose flour

1 can (14 1/2 oz.) ready-to-serve chicken broth, defatted*, divided

1 medium red pepper, chopped (1 cup)

3/4 cup sliced celery

7 green onions, white portions sliced, green tops cut into 3-inch lengths and reserved

2 cloves garlic, minced

1 can (15 oz.) black-eyed peas, rinsed and drained

2 medium tomatoes, chopped (2 cups)

1 can (4 oz.) diced green chilies

1/4 cup snipped fresh parsley

1 teaspoon dried thyme leaves

1/2 teaspoon pepper

1/8 teaspoon red pepper sauce

8 bone-in chicken thighs (5 oz. each), skin removed

1/2 teaspoon Cajun seasoning

1 pkg. (10 oz.) frozen cut okra, defrosted

8 servings

*Defat broth by chilling 4 hours; skim and discard solidified fat from surface.

1 Heat oven to 400°F. Sprinkle flour evenly into 8-inch square baking pan. Bake for 10 to 15 minutes, or until deep golden brown, stirring every 5 minutes. Set aside.

2 Combine 1/2 cup broth, the red pepper, celery, white portions of onions and the garlic in 4-quart Dutch oven. Cook over medium-high heat for 4 to 5 minutes, or until vegetables are tender-crisp, stirring occasionally. Stir in flour. Blend in remaining broth, the peas, tomatoes, chilies, parsley, thyme, pepper and red pepper sauce.

3 Rub chicken with Cajun seasoning. Add to gumbo. Bring gumbo to boil over high heat. Cover. Reduce heat to low. Simmer for 25 to 35 minutes, or until meat near bone on chicken is no longer pink and juices run clear. (If desired, remove chicken and cut meat from bones. Discard bones. Return meat to gumbo.)

4 Stir in reserved onion tops and the okra. Cook for 4 to 5 minutes, or until onion tops are wilted and mixture thickens slightly. Serve over hot cooked rice and sprinkle with filé powder, if desired. (Filé powder is a seasoning made from dried sassafras leaves, used to flavor and thicken Creole dishes.)

Nutrition Facts	Amount/serving	%DV*	Amount/serving	%DV*	Menu Planning Guide
Serving Size approximately 1 cup (282g)	Total Fat 7g	10%	Total Carbohydrate 20g	7%	One serving of this recipe provides:
	Saturated Fat 2g	9%	Dietary Fiber 6g	23%	1 Meat, Poultry & Fish
Servings per Recipe 8	Cholesterol 56mg	19%	Sugars 4g		1 Vegetable
Calories 233 Calories from Fat 59	Sodium 320mg	13%	Protein 23g		

Vitamin A 15% • Vitamin C 70% • Calcium 8% • Iron 20%
*Percent Daily Values (DV) are based on a 2000 calorie diet.

Diet Exchanges:
• 2 lean meat • 1 starch • 1 vegetable

White Bean & Chicken Chili

Serve with corn bread and sliced fresh tomatoes

2 boneless whole chicken breasts (8 to 10 oz. each), split in half, skin removed

1 cup finely chopped green pepper

1 medium onion, chopped (1 cup)

1 tablespoon vegetable oil

3 tablespoons all-purpose flour

1 cup water

2 cans (15½ oz. each) white kidney beans (cannellini), rinsed and drained

1 can (14½ oz.) ready-to-serve chicken broth

1 cup frozen corn

1 can (4 oz.) chopped green chilies

2 tablespoons fresh lime juice

1 jar (2 oz.) diced pimientos, drained (optional)

2 teaspoons ground cumin

8 servings

1 Heat oven to 350°F. Place chicken in 8-inch square baking dish. Cover with foil. Bake for 25 to 30 minutes, or until meat is no longer pink and juices run clear. Drain. Cool slightly. Shred chicken. Set aside.

2 Combine pepper, onion and oil in 4-quart saucepan. Cook over medium heat for 5½ to 7 minutes, or until vegetables are tender, stirring occasionally. Stir in flour. Blend in water.

3 Add chicken and remaining ingredients. Mix well. Cook for 13 to 16 minutes, or until chili is hot and slightly thickened, stirring occasionally. Top each serving with crushed tortilla chips, if desired.

Microwave tip: Place chicken on roasting rack or in 8-inch square baking dish. Cover with wax paper. Microwave at High for 4 to 9 minutes, or until meat is no longer pink and juices run clear, rearranging once. Continue as directed.

Nutrition Facts

Serving Size approximately 1 cup (294g)
Servings per Recipe 8
Calories 198
Calories from Fat 35

Amount/serving	%DV*	Amount/serving	%DV*
Total Fat 4g	6%	Total Carbohydrate 28g	9%
Saturated Fat 1g	4%	Dietary Fiber 7g	28%
Cholesterol 30mg	10%	Sugars 5g	
Sodium 393mg	16%	Protein 20g	

Vitamin A 6% • Vitamin C 30% • Calcium 6% • Iron 15%
*Percent Daily Values (DV) are based on a 2000 calorie diet.

Menu Planning Guide

One serving of this recipe provides:
1 Meat, Poultry & Fish
½ Vegetable

Diet Exchanges:

1½ lean meat • 1½ starch • ½ vegetable

Southern Succotash Soup

Serve with spinach salad and sourdough bread

1 cup dried black-eyed peas
½ cup dried lima beans
½ cup dried red kidney beans
10 cups water, divided
1 tablespoon olive oil
2 medium carrots, sliced (1 cup)
2 stalks celery, sliced (1 cup)
1 medium onion, sliced (1 cup)
3-lb. whole broiler-fryer chicken, cut into
    8 pieces, skin removed
    Cajun Seasoning Mix*
2 cups frozen corn
1 pkg. (9 oz.) frozen lima beans

14 servings

*Cajun Seasoning Mix

1 tablespoon dried parsley flakes
1½ teaspoons dried oregano leaves
1½ teaspoons dried thyme leaves
1 teaspoon paprika
1 tablespoon instant chicken bouillon granules
1 teaspoon ground cumin
½ teaspoon instant minced garlic
½ teaspoon freshly ground pepper
¼ to ½ teaspoon cayenne
1 teaspoon salt

1 Rinse and drain dried peas and beans; remove any grit and discolored or shriveled legumes. Place in 3-quart saucepan. Add 4 cups water. Bring to boil over medium-high heat, stirring occasionally. Boil for 2 minutes. Cover. Remove from heat. Let stand for 1 hour. Drain and discard liquid from peas and beans. Rinse with warm water. Drain. Set aside.

2 Place oil in 6-quart Dutch oven or stockpot. Heat over medium-high heat. Add carrots, celery and onion. Cook for 4 to 5 minutes, or until vegetables are tender, stirring frequently.

3 Reduce heat to medium. Stir in prepared peas and beans, the chicken, seasoning mix and remaining 6 cups water. Bring mixture to boil, stirring frequently. Reduce heat to low and simmer, partially covered, for 1½ hours, stirring occasionally.

4 Remove chicken from soup. Cool slightly. Cut meat from bones. Discard bones. Add chicken, corn and frozen lima beans to soup. Continue to cook, partially covered, for 30 to 45 minutes, or until beans are softened and soup is hot, stirring occasionally.

Nutrition Facts	Amount/serving	%DV*	Amount/serving	%DV*
Serving Size 1 cup (340g)	Total Fat 4g	7%	Total Carbohydrate 28g	9%
Servings per Recipe 14	Saturated Fat 1g	5%	Dietary Fiber 6g	25%
Calories 200	Cholesterol 30mg	9%	Sugars 4g	
Calories from Fat 40	Sodium 206mg	9%	Protein 16g	

Vitamin A 30% • Vitamin C 6% • Calcium 8% • Iron 15%
*Percent Daily Values (DV) are based on a 2000 calorie diet.

Menu Planning Guide

One serving of this recipe provides:
1 Meat, Poultry & Fish
½ Vegetable

Diet Exchanges:

1 lean meat • 2 starch

Chicken Dinner Soup

Serve with corn bread

8 cups water

3 - lb. *whole broiler-fryer chicken, quartered,*
    skin removed

3 *stalks celery, cut into 2 x ¼-inch strips*
    (1½ cups)

3 *medium carrots, cut into 2 x ¼-inch strips*
    (1½ cups)

6 *new potatoes, cut into ½-inch chunks*
    (1½ cups)

1 *small leek, cut into 2 x ¼-inch strips (1 cup)*

1½ *teaspoons dried tarragon leaves*

1 *teaspoon freshly ground black pepper*

1 *teaspoon salt*

10 servings

1 Combine water and chicken pieces in 6-quart Dutch oven or stockpot. Bring to boil over high heat. Reduce heat to low. Cover. Simmer for 1 hour 15 minutes, skimming occasionally.

2 Remove chicken from broth. Chill broth, covered, at least 4 hours. Cut meat from bones. Discard bones. Coarsely shred chicken. Wrap in plastic wrap. Chill.

3 Skim and discard solidified fat from top of broth. Strain broth. In 6-quart Dutch oven or stockpot, combine broth, chicken and remaining ingredients. Bring to boil over high heat. Reduce heat to medium-low. Simmer for 20 to 30 minutes, or until potatoes are tender.

Nutrition Facts	Amount/serving	%DV*	Amount/serving	%DV*
Serving Size approximately 1 cup (315g)	Total Fat 3g	5%	Total Carbohydrate 9g	3%
	Saturated Fat 1g	5%	Dietary Fiber 2g	7%
Servings per Recipe 10	Cholesterol 41mg	14%	Sugars 2g	
	Sodium 281mg	12%	Protein 14g	
Calories 124 Calories from Fat 31	Vitamin A 110% • Vitamin C 8% • Calcium 4% • Iron 6%			
	*Percent Daily Values (DV) are based on a 2000 calorie diet.			

Menu Planning Guide

One serving of this recipe provides:

1 Meat, Poultry & Fish
1 Vegetable

Diet Exchanges:

2 lean meat • 1 vegetable

Spicy Manhattan Clam Chowder

Serve with a sourdough roll

1 cup cubed red potatoes (¼-inch cubes)

⅓ cup chopped onion

¼ cup grated carrot

¼ cup water

1 tablespoon margarine

2 cans (14½ oz. each) whole tomatoes, undrained, cut up

1 can (6½ oz.) minced clams, undrained

¾ cup spicy vegetable juice

2 tablespoons catsup

2 tablespoons snipped fresh parsley

1 bay leaf

¼ to ½ teaspoon red pepper sauce

¼ teaspoon dried thyme leaves

⅛ teaspoon pepper

6 servings

1 Combine potatoes, onion, carrot, water and margarine in 3-quart saucepan. Cook over medium heat for 8 to 10 minutes, or until vegetables are tender, stirring frequently. (If vegetables begin to stick, add additional ¼ cup water and continue cooking.)

2 Stir in remaining ingredients. Bring mixture to boil over high heat. Cover. Reduce heat to low. Simmer for 10 to 15 minutes, or until chowder is hot and flavors are blended, stirring occasionally. Remove and discard bay leaf before serving.

Microwave tip: Omit water. In 2-quart casserole, combine potatoes, onion, carrot and margarine. Cover. Microwave at High for 5 to 6 minutes, or until vegetables are tender, stirring once. Stir in remaining ingredients. Re-cover. Microwave at 70% (Medium High) for 10 to 14 minutes, or until chowder is hot and flavors are blended, stirring once. Remove and discard bay leaf before serving.

Nutrition Facts	Amount/serving	%DV*	Amount/serving	%DV*
Serving Size approximately 1 cup (254g)	Total Fat 3g	4%	Total Carbohydrate 16g	5%
Servings per Recipe 6	Saturated Fat <1g	2%	Dietary Fiber 2g	8%
Calories 106	Cholesterol 10mg	3%	Sugars 6g	
Calories from Fat 24	Sodium 451mg	19%	Protein 6g	

Vitamin A 60% • Vitamin C 60% • Calcium 6% • Iron 35%

*Percent Daily Values (DV) are based on a 2000 calorie diet.

Menu Planning Guide

One serving of this recipe provides:

1½ Vegetable

Diet Exchanges:

2 lean meat • ½ starch • 1 vegetable

Seafood Stew

Serve with a crisp green salad

2 cups French bread cubes (1 x 1 x
    1/2-inch cubes)

3/4 teaspoon dried thyme leaves, divided

1/4 teaspoon garlic powder

1 can (14 1/2 oz.) whole tomatoes, undrained

2 large leeks, halved lengthwise and sliced
    (2 cups)

2 cups water, divided

1 medium carrot, thinly sliced (1/2 cup)

3 cloves garlic, minced

1 1/2 cups dry white wine or ready-to-serve
    chicken broth

1/2 cup clam juice (optional)

1 tablespoon sugar

1/4 teaspoon fennel seed, crushed

1/4 teaspoon freshly ground pepper

1 bay leaf

12 frozen medium mussels, scrubbed
    and debearded

8 oz. fresh medium sea scallops

8 oz. fresh medium shrimp, shelled and
    deveined

8 servings

Note: This is a broth-type stew.

1 Heat oven to 375°F. Spread bread cubes on baking sheet. Spray bread cubes with nonstick vegetable cooking spray. In small bowl, combine 1/4 teaspoon thyme and the garlic powder. Sprinkle mixture evenly over bread cubes. Bake for 7 to 8 minutes, or until light golden brown, stirring once or twice. Set croutons aside.

2 Process tomatoes in food processor or blender until smooth. Set aside. In 3-quart saucepan, combine leeks, 1/2 cup water, the carrot and garlic. Cover. Cook over high heat for 4 1/2 to 6 minutes, or until carrot is tender-crisp. Stir in remaining 1/2 teaspoon thyme, the processed tomatoes, remaining 1 1/2 cups water, the wine, clam juice, sugar, fennel, pepper and bay leaf. Bring mixture to boil. Reduce heat to low. Simmer, uncovered, for 20 minutes, stirring occasionally.

3 Stir in mussels and scallops. Cover. Increase heat to medium. Cook for 4 to 5 minutes, or until mussels are hot and shells are open. Stir in shrimp. Cook, uncovered, for 2 to 4 minutes, or until shrimp and scallops are firm and opaque, stirring occasionally. Remove and discard bay leaf. Sprinkle each serving with 1/4 cup croutons.

Nutrition Facts	Amount/serving	%DV*	Amount/serving	%DV*
Serving Size approximately 1 cup (240g) Servings per Recipe 8	Total Fat 3g	5%	Total Carbohydrate 16g	5%
	Saturated Fat 1g	3%	Dietary Fiber 2g	8%
	Cholesterol 60mg	20%	Sugars 7g	
Calories 180 Calories from Fat 27	Sodium 395mg	16%	Protein 19g	

Vitamin A 50% • Vitamin C 25% • Calcium 6% • Iron 25%
*Percent Daily Values (DV) are based on a 2000 calorie diet.

Menu Planning Guide

One serving of this recipe provides:
1 Meat, Poultry & Fish
1 Vegetable
1/2 Bread, Cereal, Rice & Pasta

Diet Exchanges:

2 lean meat • 1/2 starch • 1 vegetable

Bouillabaisse

Serve with endive and onion salad

1 tablespoon olive oil

3 large leeks, cut in half lengthwise and sliced
  (3 cups)

1 small onion, chopped (½ cup)

¼ cup dry white wine

4 cloves garlic, minced

4 medium tomatoes, peeled, seeded and chopped
  (4 cups)

1 tablespoon snipped fresh tarragon leaves

1 tablespoon snipped fresh parsley

2 bay leaves

½ teaspoon salt

½ teaspoon pepper

¼ teaspoon saffron threads, crushed

2 cups ready-to-serve chicken broth

2 cups water

8 oz. fresh or frozen mussels, scrubbed and
  debearded

8 oz. fresh halibut, cut into ½-inch chunks

8 oz. fresh or frozen bay scallops

8 oz. fresh or frozen large shrimp

12 servings

Tip: Add red pepper sauce to individual servings, if desired.

1 Heat oil over medium heat in 6-quart Dutch oven or stockpot. Add leeks, onion, wine and garlic. Cook for 5 to 7 minutes, or until vegetables are tender, stirring occasionally. Stir in tomatoes, tarragon, parsley, bay leaves, salt, pepper and saffron. Cook for 10 minutes, stirring occasionally.

2 Stir in broth and water. Bring to boil over medium-high heat. Stir in mussels, halibut and scallops. Return to boil. Boil for 10 to 15 minutes, or until mussels are open and flavors are blended, stirring occasionally.

3 Stir in shrimp. Cook for 1 to 2 minutes, or until shrimp are firm and opaque. Remove from heat. Remove and discard bay leaves. Serve bouillabaisse over thick slices of toasted French bread, if desired.

Nutrition Facts	Amount/serving	%DV*	Amount/serving	%DV*
Serving Size 1 cup (245g)	Total Fat 3g	5%	Total Carbohydrate 9g	3%
Servings per Recipe 12	Saturated Fat <1g	3%	Dietary Fiber 2g	8%
Calories 115	Cholesterol 45mg	15%	Sugars 3g	
Calories from Fat 28	Sodium 330mg	14%	Protein 13g	

Vitamin A 15% • Vitamin C 35% • Calcium 4% • Iron 15%
*Percent Daily Values (DV) are based on a 2000 calorie diet.

Menu Planning Guide
One serving of this recipe provides:
1 Meat, Poultry & Fish
1 Vegetable

Diet Exchanges:
1½ lean meat • 1 vegetable

Jambalaya

Serve with cooked collard greens and a crusty French roll

1 tablespoon vegetable oil

1 boneless whole chicken breast (8 to 10 oz.),
    skin removed, cut into 1-inch pieces

1 medium onion, chopped (1 cup)

¾ cup chopped green pepper

1 stalk celery, sliced (½ cup)

2 jalapeño peppers, seeded and finely
    chopped

2 cloves garlic, minced

1 lb. fresh medium shrimp, shelled and
    deveined

2 cans (14½ oz. each) diced tomatoes,
    undrained

2 cups cooked long-grain white rice

1 teaspoon cayenne

1 teaspoon dried thyme leaves

¾ teaspoon salt

¼ teaspoon pepper

8 servings

1 Heat oil in 6-quart Dutch oven or stock-pot over medium heat. Add chicken, onion, green pepper, celery, jalapeños and garlic. Cook for 5 to 7 minutes, or until meat is no longer pink and vegetables are tender, stirring occasionally.

2 Add shrimp. Cook for 3 to 5 minutes, or until shrimp are firm and opaque, stirring frequently. Stir in remaining ingredients. Bring to boil. Cover. Reduce heat to low. Simmer for 20 minutes to blend flavors.

Nutrition Facts	Amount/serving	%DV*	Amount/serving	%DV*
Serving Size approximately 1 cup (274g)	Total Fat 3g	5%	Total Carbohydrate 23g	8%
	Saturated Fat 1g	4%	Dietary Fiber 2g	9%
Servings per Recipe 8	Cholesterol 98mg	33%	Sugars 5g	
Calories 197 Calories from Fat 31	Sodium 485mg	20%	Protein 18g	

Vitamin A 20% • Vitamin C 90% • Calcium 6% • Iron 20%

*Percent Daily Values (DV) are based on a 2000 calorie diet.

Menu Planning Guide
One serving of this recipe provides:
1 Meat, Poultry & Fish
1 Vegetable
½ Bread, Cereal, Rice & Pasta

Diet Exchanges:
1½ lean meat • 1 starch • 1 vegetable

Black Bean Chili

Serve with corn bread, chicken taco
or South of the Border Muffuletta (p 90)

4 cans (15 oz. each) black beans, rinsed
   and drained, divided
1 can (14½ oz.) ready-to-serve chicken broth
1 small onion, chopped (½ cup)
1 stalk celery, thinly sliced (½ cup)
⅓ cup chopped green pepper
2 cloves garlic, minced
2 teaspoons olive oil
1 can (14½ oz.) whole tomatoes, undrained
   and cut up
2 teaspoons chili powder
½ teaspoon ground cumin
½ teaspoon dried oregano leaves
¼ teaspoon salt
½ cup chopped seeded tomato
½ cup sliced green onions
2 tablespoons plus 2 teaspoons plain nonfat
   or low-fat yogurt

8 servings

1 Place 3 cups beans and the broth in food processor or blender. Process until smooth. Set aside.

2 Combine onion, celery, pepper, garlic and oil in 3-quart saucepan. Cook over medium heat for 8 to 10 minutes, or until vegetables are tender, stirring frequently. Add processed beans, remaining beans, the canned tomatoes, chili powder, cumin, oregano and salt. Mix well.

3 Bring to boil over high heat, stirring occasionally. Reduce heat to low. Cook for 10 to 15 minutes, or until chili is hot and flavors are blended, stirring occasionally. Garnish each serving with 1 tablespoon each chopped tomato and green onion, and 1 teaspoon yogurt.

Nutrition Facts	Amount/serving	%DV*	Amount/serving	%DV*
Serving Size approximately 1 cup (335g)	Total Fat 3g	4%	Total Carbohydrate 50g	17%
Servings per Recipe 8	Saturated Fat 1g	3%	Dietary Fiber 18g	72%
Calories 290	Cholesterol <1mg	0%	Sugars 7g	
Calories from Fat 25	Sodium 335mg	14%	Protein 19g	

Vitamin A 15% • Vitamin C 30% • Calcium 10% • Iron 25%
*Percent Daily Values (DV) are based on a 2000 calorie diet.

Menu Planning Guide
One serving of this recipe provides:
1 Meat, Poultry & Fish
1 Vegetable

Diet Exchanges:
3 starch • 1 vegetable

Tortellini Stew

Serve with a tossed green salad and garlic toast

2 teaspoons olive oil

8 oz. fresh mushrooms, sliced (3 cups)

1 medium onion, chopped (1 cup)

1 clove garlic, minced

2 medium tomatoes, chopped (2 cups)

1½ cups water

1 can (8 oz.) no-salt-added tomato sauce

½ cup thick and chunky salsa

2 tablespoons snipped fresh basil leaves

1½ teaspoons instant beef bouillon granules

¼ teaspoon freshly ground pepper

1 pkg. (9 oz.) uncooked fresh cheese tortellini

6 servings

1 Heat oil in 3-quart saucepan over medium-high heat. Add mushrooms, onion and garlic. Cook for 3½ to 5 minutes, or until vegetables are tender, stirring frequently. Stir in remaining ingredients, except tortellini. Bring to boil.

2 Stir in tortellini. Cover. Reduce heat to medium-low. Simmer for 6 to 8 minutes, or until tortellini are tender, stirring occasionally. Sprinkle each serving with shredded fresh Parmesan cheese, if desired.

Nutrition Facts	Amount/serving	%DV*	Amount/serving	%DV*
Serving Size approximately 1 cup (293g)	Total Fat 5g	8%	Total Carbohydrate 32g	11%
Servings per Recipe 6	Saturated Fat 2g	8%	Dietary Fiber 4g	16%
Calories 201	Cholesterol 23mg	8%	Sugars 5g	
Calories from Fat 47	Sodium 499mg	21%	Protein 9g	

Vitamin A 20% • Vitamin C 40% • Calcium 10% • Iron 15%

*Percent Daily Values (DV) are based on a 2000 calorie diet.

Menu Planning Guide

One serving of this recipe provides:
  2 Vegetable
1½ Bread, Cereal, Rice & Pasta

Diet Exchanges:

½ lean meat • 1½ starch • 2 vegetable

Split Pea Soup

Serve with Light Cobb Salad (p 80)
or Barbecued Chicken Sandwich (p 88)

1 can (14½ oz.) ready-to-serve chicken broth

1 cup dried green or yellow split peas,
   rinsed and drained

3 tablespoons snipped fresh sage leaves or
   1 tablespoon dried sage leaves

3 cups water

12 oz. peeled red potatoes, cut into ½-inch
   cubes (2 cups)

2 medium carrots, chopped (1 cup)

½ teaspoon freshly ground pepper

6 servings

1 Combine broth, peas and sage in 4-quart saucepan. Bring to boil over high heat. Remove from heat. Cover. Let stand for 45 minutes.

2 Add remaining ingredients. Bring to boil over medium-high heat. Reduce heat to low. Simmer soup, partially covered, for 45 minutes to 1 hour, or until peas are tender, stirring occasionally.

Nutrition Facts	Amount/serving	%DV*	Amount/serving	%DV*
Serving Size 1 cup (223g)	Total Fat 1g	1%	Total Carbohydrate 30g	10%
	Saturated Fat 0g	1%	Dietary Fiber 9g	34%
Servings per Recipe 6	Cholesterol 0mg	0%	Sugars 4g	
Calories 164	Sodium 238mg	10%	Protein 9g	
Calories from Fat 10	Vitamin A 120% • Vitamin C 8% • Calcium 4% • Iron 10%			
	*Percent Daily Values (DV) are based on a 2000 calorie diet.			

Menu Planning Guide

One serving of this recipe provides:

1 Vegetable

Diet Exchanges:

2 starch

Tortilla Soup

Serve with South of the Border Muffuletta (p 90)
or Black Bean Tortilla Pockets (p 101)

1 tablespoon vegetable oil
1 medium onion, chopped (1 cup)
1 stalk celery, thinly sliced (1/2 cup)
1 jalapeño pepper, seeded and finely chopped
2 cloves garlic, minced
1 can (28 oz.) whole tomatoes, undrained
   and cut up
2 1/2 cups water
1 can (15 1/2 oz.) pinto beans, rinsed and
   drained
1 cup frozen corn
2 to 3 teaspoons chili powder
1 teaspoon cumin seed, crushed
1 tablespoon snipped fresh cilantro leaves
1/2 cup coarsely crushed baked tortilla chips

8 servings

Tip: Use scissors to cut up tomatoes in the can.

1 Heat oil in 4-quart saucepan over medium heat. Add onion, celery, pepper and garlic. Cook for 3 to 4 minutes, or until vegetables are tender, stirring frequently.

2 Stir in tomatoes, water, beans, corn, chili powder and cumin seed. Bring to boil. Reduce heat to low. Cover. Simmer for 15 minutes to blend flavors. Remove from heat.

3 Stir in cilantro. Just before serving, sprinkle 1 tablespoon chips over each serving.

Nutrition Facts	Amount/serving	%DV*	Amount/serving	%DV*
Serving Size approximately 1 cup (285g)	Total Fat 3g	4%	Total Carbohydrate 25g	8%
	Saturated Fat <1g	2%	Dietary Fiber 5g	21%
Servings per Recipe 8	Cholesterol 0mg	0%	Sugars 6g	
	Sodium 300mg	13%	Protein 6g	
Calories 134 Calories from Fat 23	Vitamin A 20% • Vitamin C 50% • Calcium 6% • Iron 10%			
	*Percent Daily Values (DV) are based on a 2000 calorie diet.			

Menu Planning Guide

One serving of this recipe provides:
1 Vegetable
1 1/2 Bread, Cereal, Rice & Pasta

Diet Exchanges:

1 1/2 vegetable

Tofu Chili

Serve with Black Bean Tortilla Pockets (p 101) or corn bread

1 tablespoon vegetable oil
2 medium carrots, sliced (1 cup)
1 medium onion, chopped (1 cup)
1 stalk celery, sliced (1/2 cup)
1/2 cup chopped green pepper
2 jalapeño peppers, seeded and finely chopped
2 cloves garlic, minced
4 medium tomatoes, seeded and chopped
    (4 cups)
1 can (15 oz.) dark red kidney beans, rinsed
    and drained
1 cup water
2 tablespoons tomato paste
1 tablespoon chili powder
2 teaspoons packed brown sugar
1 teaspoon ground cumin
1/2 teaspoon salt
1/2 teaspoon ground cinnamon (optional)
1 pkg. (10 1/2 oz.) extra-firm tofu, drained,
    cut into 3/4-inch cubes
1 tablespoon snipped fresh cilantro leaves

6 servings

1 Heat oil in 4-quart saucepan over medium heat. Add carrots, onion, celery, peppers and garlic. Cook for 6 to 7 minutes, or until vegetables are tender, stirring frequently.

2 Stir in remaining ingredients, except tofu and cilantro. Bring to boil over high heat. Gently stir in tofu. Reduce heat to medium-low. Simmer for 45 minutes to 1 hour, or until chili is thickened, stirring occasionally. Remove from heat. Stir in cilantro.

Nutrition Facts	Amount/serving	%DV*	Amount/serving	%DV*
Serving Size approximately 1 cup (384g)	Total Fat 7g	11%	Total Carbohydrate 35g	12%
	Saturated Fat 1g	5%	Dietary Fiber 9g	35%
Servings per Recipe 6	Cholesterol 0mg	0%	Sugars 11g	
Calories 245 Calories from Fat 67	Sodium 431mg	18%	Protein 15g	
	Vitamin A 150% • Vitamin C 100% • Calcium 15% • Iron 45%			
	*Percent Daily Values (DV) are based on a 2000 calorie diet.			

Menu Planning Guide

One serving of this recipe provides:
1 Meat, Poultry & Fish
3 Vegetable

Diet Exchanges:

1/2 medium-fat meat • 1 1/2 starch • 3 vegetable • 1/2 fat

Ethiopian Lentil Stew

Serve with pita bread and Fruited Couscous Salad (p 77)

Spice Blend:

2 teaspoons paprika

1 teaspoon onion powder

½ to 1 teaspoon cayenne

½ teaspoon dried basil leaves

½ teaspoon salt

¼ teaspoon garlic powder

¼ teaspoon ground ginger

¼ teaspoon ground allspice

¼ teaspoon turmeric

   Dash ground cumin

   Dash ground cardamom

7 cups water, divided

1 cup uncooked brown lentils, rinsed and drained

⅓ cup finely chopped onion

2 teaspoons olive oil

1 clove garlic, minced

4 servings

Tip: This ethnic stew is thicker than traditional stews. It is commonly eaten with flatbread that is used as a utensil to scoop up the mixture.

Spice blend can be used to season poultry, chili or taco meat.

1 Combine spice blend ingredients in small bowl. Set aside. In 3-quart saucepan, bring 6 cups water to boil over high heat. Add lentils. Reduce heat to low. Simmer for 35 to 45 minutes, or until lentils are tender. Drain. With fork or potato masher, coarsely mash lentils. Set aside.

2 Spray 10-inch nonstick skillet with non-stick vegetable cooking spray. Heat skillet over medium heat. Add onion. Cook for 2 to 3 minutes, or until tender and light brown, stirring frequently. Reduce heat to low. Stir in spice blend, oil and garlic. Cook for 1 minute, stirring constantly.

3 Stir in mashed lentils and ½ cup water. Simmer for 15 minutes, stirring occasionally. Stir in remaining ½ cup water. Simmer for additional 15 minutes to blend flavors, stirring occasionally and adding additional water, if desired, to reach desired consistency. Serve stew warm with flatbread, soft tortillas, chips or raw vegetables, if desired.

Nutrition Facts	Amount/serving	%DV*	Amount/serving	%DV*	Menu Planning Guide
Serving Size approximately ½ cup (210g)	Total Fat 3g	5%	Total Carbohydrate 29g	10%	One serving of this recipe provides:
Servings per Recipe 4	Saturated Fat <1g	2%	Dietary Fiber 7g	26%	½ Meat, Poultry & Fish
Calories 185	Cholesterol 0mg	0%	Sugars 4g		
Calories from Fat 27	Sodium 273mg	11%	Protein 12g		
	Vitamin A 15% • Vitamin C 6% • Calcium 4% • Iron 25%				Diet Exchanges:
	*Percent Daily Values (DV) are based on a 2000 calorie diet.				2 starch

Mexican Corn Chowder

Serve with Denver Omelet Sandwiches (p 106)

1 small onion, chopped (½ cup)

⅓ cup chopped green pepper

1 clove garlic, minced

1 can (10¾ oz.) condensed chicken broth

1 pkg. (10 oz.) frozen corn

1 medium tomato, seeded and chopped (1 cup)

1 cup water

2 tablespoons canned chopped green chilies

1 teaspoon dried parsley flakes

¼ teaspoon salt

¼ teaspoon ground cumin

⅛ teaspoon chili powder

4 servings

1 Spray 2-quart saucepan with nonstick vegetable cooking spray. Add onion, pepper and garlic. Cook over medium heat for 5 to 7 minutes, or until vegetables are tender, stirring frequently. (If vegetables begin to stick, move them to one side and spray saucepan with nonstick vegetable cooking spray.)

2 Stir in remaining ingredients. Bring to boil over high heat. Reduce heat to low and simmer, covered, for 6 to 10 minutes, or until chowder is hot and flavors are blended, stirring occasionally.

Microwave tip: In 2-quart casserole, combine onion, pepper and garlic. Cover. Microwave at High for 5 to 7 minutes, or until vegetables are tender, stirring once or twice. Stir in remaining ingredients. Re-cover. Microwave at High for 8 to 12 minutes, or until chowder is hot and flavors are blended, stirring once or twice.

Nutrition Facts

Serving Size 1 cup (281g)
Servings per Recipe 4
Calories 93
Calories from Fat 6

Amount/serving	%DV*	Amount/serving	%DV*
Total Fat 1g	1%	Total Carbohydrate 20g	7%
Saturated Fat <1g	0%	Dietary Fiber 3g	12%
Cholesterol 0mg	0%	Sugars 4g	
Sodium 393mg	16%	Protein 4g	

Vitamin A 10% • Vitamin C 30% • Calcium 2% • Iron 6%
*Percent Daily Values (DV) are based on a 2000 calorie diet.

Menu Planning Guide

One serving of this recipe provides:
  2 Vegetable

Diet Exchanges:

1 starch • 1 vegetable

Italian Vegetable Soup

Serve with Hearty Tuna Sandwiches (p 95)
or sliced tomato salad with Spinach & Shallot Dressing (p 85)

3 cups fresh vegetables, any combination
   (broccoli, cauliflower, onions, red and green
   peppers, cut into 1-inch pieces; carrots,
   cut into 1/4-inch slices; snow pea pods)
2 cloves garlic, minced
1 1/4 cups water, divided
1 can (10 1/2 oz.) condensed beef consommé
1/2 cup dry red wine
1 teaspoon Italian seasoning
2 oz. uncooked capellini (angel hair spaghetti),
   broken into 2-inch lengths

4 servings

1 Combine vegetables, garlic and 1/2 cup water in 2-quart saucepan. Cover. Cook over medium heat for 8 to 12 minutes, or until vegetables are tender-crisp, stirring occasionally.

2 Stir in consommé, remaining 3/4 cup water, the wine, Italian seasoning and capellini. Bring to boil over high heat. Reduce heat to medium-low. Simmer, uncovered, for 5 to 10 minutes, or until vegetables and capellini are tender, stirring occasionally.

Nutrition Facts	Amount/serving	%DV*	Amount/serving	%DV*
Serving Size approximately 1 cup (281g)	Total Fat <1g	0%	Total Carbohydrate 21g	7%
	Saturated Fat <1g	0%	Dietary Fiber 3g	12%
Servings per Recipe 4	Cholesterol 0mg	0%	Sugars 5g	
	Sodium 405mg	17%	Protein 9g	
Calories 122 Calories from Fat 3	Vitamin A 70% • Vitamin C 90% • Calcium 4% • Iron 8%			
	*Percent Daily Values (DV) are based on a 2000 calorie diet.			

Menu Planning Guide

One serving of this recipe provides:
1 1/2 Vegetable
1 Bread, Cereal, Rice & Pasta

Diet Exchanges:

1/2 starch • 2 vegetable

Potato-Leek Soup

Serve with TLT's with Herbed Mayonnaise (p 109) or Egg Salad Sandwiches (p 87)

 2 *large leeks, cut into ¼-inch slices (2 cups)*

 ½ *cup grated carrot*

 1 *tablespoon margarine*

 1 *clove garlic, minced*

3½ *cups water*

 3 *cups cubed red potatoes (¼-inch cubes)*

 1 *tablespoon instant chicken bouillon granules*

 1 *can (12 oz.) evaporated skim milk*

 ¼ *to ½ teaspoon white pepper*

 2 *tablespoons snipped fresh parsley*

6 servings

1 Spray 3-quart saucepan with nonstick vegetable cooking spray. Add leeks, carrot, margarine and garlic. Cook over medium heat for 4 to 6 minutes, or until vegetables are tender-crisp, stirring frequently. Add water, potatoes and bouillon. Bring to boil over high heat. Cover. Reduce heat to low. Simmer for 3 to 5 minutes, or until potatoes are tender. Remove from heat.

2 Place 3 cups of mixture into food processor or blender. Process until smooth. Return processed mixture to saucepan. Stir in milk and pepper. Cook, uncovered, over high heat for 4 to 6 minutes, or until soup is hot, stirring occasionally. Stir in parsley.

Nutrition Facts	Amount/serving	%DV*	Amount/serving	%DV*	Menu Planning Guide
Serving Size approximately 1 cup (319g)	Total Fat 2g	3%	Total Carbohydrate 26g	9%	One serving of this recipe provides:
	Saturated Fat <1g	2%	Dietary Fiber 3g	12%	½ Milk, Yogurt & Cheese 2 Vegetable
Servings per Recipe 6	Cholesterol 2mg	1%	Sugars 8g		
Calories 147	Sodium 554mg	23%	Protein 6g		
Calories from Fat 20	Vitamin A 45% • Vitamin C 25% • Calcium 20% • Iron 6%				Diet Exchanges:
	*Percent Daily Values (DV) are based on a 2000 calorie diet.				½ skim milk • 1 starch • 1 vegetable

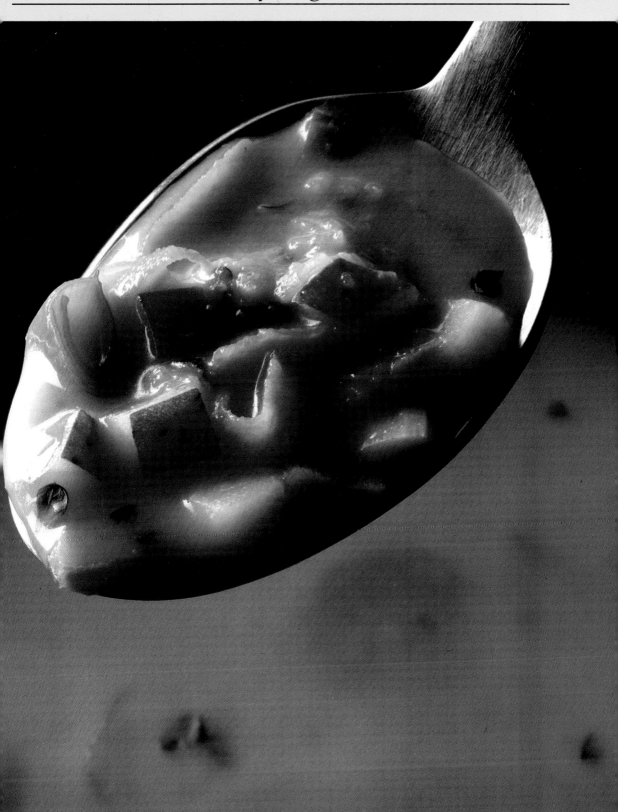

Hearty Vegetable-Barley Soup

Serve with Crab & Shallot Salad (p 83) and a crusty French roll

3 cups water, divided
2 medium carrots, sliced (1 cup)
1 stalk celery, sliced (½ cup)
½ cup coarsely chopped green pepper
1 small onion, chopped (½ cup)
½ cup sliced fresh mushrooms
1 can (14½ oz.) diced tomatoes, undrained
½ cup uncooked quick-cooking barley
1 small zucchini, cut into ¼-inch slices
   (½ cup)
1½ teaspoons instant beef bouillon granules
1 teaspoon dried rosemary leaves, crushed
½ teaspoon dried oregano leaves
½ teaspoon pepper

6 servings

1 Combine 1 cup water, the carrots, celery, green pepper, onion and mushrooms in 3-quart saucepan. Cover. Cook over high heat for 8 to 10 minutes, or until vegetables are tender, stirring occasionally.

2 Stir in remaining 2 cups water and remaining ingredients. Bring to boil. Reduce heat to low. Simmer, uncovered, for 20 to 25 minutes, or until barley is tender, stirring occasionally.

Microwave tip: In 3-quart casserole, combine ¼ cup water, the carrots, celery, green pepper, onion and mushrooms. Cover. Microwave at High for 5 to 8 minutes, or until vegetables are tender, stirring once. Stir in remaining 2¾ cups water and remaining ingredients. Re-cover. Microwave at High for 25 to 30 minutes, or until barley is tender, stirring 2 or 3 times.

Nutrition Facts	Amount/serving	%DV*	Amount/serving	%DV*	Menu Planning Guide
Serving Size approximately 1 cup (276g)	Total Fat 1g	2%	Total Carbohydrate 24g	8%	One serving of this recipe provides:
	Saturated Fat <1g	1%	Dietary Fiber 6g	23%	2 Vegetable
Servings per Recipe 6	Cholesterol 0mg	0%	Sugars 5g		½ Bread, Cereal, Rice & Pasta
Calories 110 Calories from Fat 9	Sodium 372mg	16%	Protein 4g		

Vitamin A 120% • Vitamin C 35% • Calcium 4% • Iron 8%
*Percent Daily Values (DV) are based on a 2000 calorie diet.

Diet Exchanges:
½ starch • 2 vegetable

Sweet Potato-Tomato Soup

*Serve with Meatball Hoagies (p 96)
or Light Cobb Salad (p 80)*

3 cups cubed peeled sweet potatoes
    (1/2-inch cubes)

2 cups water

2 teaspoons olive oil

1 small onion, chopped (1/2 cup)

1 to 3 teaspoons snipped fresh rosemary leaves

2 cloves garlic, minced

2 cans (14 1/2 oz. each) whole tomatoes,
    undrained and coarsely chopped

1/4 teaspoon pepper

6 servings

Tip: Use scissors to coarsely chop tomatoes in the can.

1 Combine potatoes and water in 3-quart saucepan. Bring to boil over high heat. Cover. Reduce heat to low. Simmer for 6 to 8 minutes, or until potatoes are tender. Remove from heat. Using slotted spoon, transfer 1 1/2 cups potatoes to food processor. Process until smooth. Return to saucepan. Set aside.

2 Heat oil over medium heat in 4-quart saucepan. Add onion. Cook for 3 to 4 minutes, or until tender, stirring frequently. Add rosemary and garlic. Cook for 1 minute, stirring constantly. Stir in potato mixture, tomatoes and pepper. Bring to boil. Reduce heat to low. Simmer for 20 minutes to blend flavors.

Nutrition Facts	Amount/serving	%DV*	Amount/serving	%DV*	Menu Planning Guide
Serving Size approximately 1 cup (398g)	Total Fat 2g	4%	Total Carbohydrate 48g	16%	One serving of this recipe provides: 2 Vegetable
Servings per Recipe 6	Saturated Fat <1g	2%	Dietary Fiber 6g	24%	
	Cholesterol 0mg	0%	Sugars 23g		
Calories 222 Calories from Fat 22	Sodium 248mg	10%	Protein 4g		
	Vitamin A 580% • Vitamin C 80% • Calcium 8% • Iron 10%				
	*Percent Daily Values (DV) are based on a 2000 calorie diet.				**Diet Exchanges:** 2 1/2 starch • 1 vegetable

Mushroom Soup

*Serve with grilled chicken and Warm New Potato Salad (p 78)
or Mediterranean Tuna Sandwich (p 104)*

5 cups sliced mixed fresh mushrooms (white
   button, shiitake, crimini, chanterelle)

¼ cup dry sherry

3 cups hot water

½ cup diagonally sliced green onions
   (1-inch lengths)

1½ teaspoons instant beef bouillon granules

1 teaspoon dried summer savory

½ teaspoon sugar

⅛ teaspoon freshly ground pepper

4 servings

1 Combine mushrooms and sherry in 3-quart saucepan. Cover. Cook over medium-high heat for 4 to 6 minutes, or just until mushrooms are tender. Stir in remaining ingredients. Bring to boil over high heat. Reduce heat to low. Simmer, uncovered, for 5 to 6 minutes, or until soup is hot and flavors are blended, stirring occasionally.

Microwave tip: In 3-quart casserole, combine mushrooms and sherry. Cover. Microwave at High for 4 to 5 minutes, or just until mushrooms are tender, stirring once. Stir in remaining ingredients. Re-cover. Microwave at High for 4 to 6 minutes, or until soup is hot and flavors are blended, stirring once.

Nutrition Facts	Amount/serving	%DV*	Amount/serving	%DV*
Serving Size approximately 1 cup (318g)	Total Fat 1g	1%	Total Carbohydrate 12g	4%
	Saturated Fat <1g	0%	Dietary Fiber 3g	12%
Servings per Recipe 4	Cholesterol 0mg	0%	Sugars 1g	
Calories 63 Calories from Fat 5	Sodium 361mg	15%	Protein 3g	

Vitamin A 2% • Vitamin C 8% • Calcium 2% • Iron 10%
*Percent Daily Values (DV) are based on a 2000 calorie diet.

Menu Planning Guide
One serving of this recipe provides:
2 Vegetable

Diet Exchanges:
2 vegetable

Sweet & Sour Pineapple Soup

Serve with egg rolls or Hearty Tuna Sandwiches (p 95)

2 cans (14½ oz. each) ready-to-serve
   chicken broth, divided
2 tablespoons cornstarch
2 tablespoons packed brown sugar
2 tablespoons white vinegar
⅛ to ¼ teaspoon crushed red pepper flakes
1 cup red and green pepper strips
   (2 x ¼-inch strips)
1 large leek, sliced (1 cup)
1 can (20 oz.) pineapple chunks in juice,
   undrained

6 servings

1 Combine 3 cups broth, the cornstarch, sugar, vinegar and red pepper flakes in 4-cup measure. Set broth mixture aside.

2 Combine pepper strips, leek and remaining broth in 3-quart saucepan. Cover. Cook over high heat for 4 to 5 minutes, or until peppers are tender-crisp, stirring occasionally.

3 Stir in broth mixture and pineapple. Reduce heat to medium. Cook for 12 to 14 minutes, or until soup is slightly thickened and translucent, stirring occasionally.

Nutrition Facts	Amount/serving	%DV*	Amount/serving	%DV*
Serving Size approximately 1 cup (282g)	Total Fat 1g	2%	Total Carbohydrate 24g	8%
	Saturated Fat <1g	1%	Dietary Fiber 2g	8%
Servings per Recipe 6	Cholesterol 0mg	0%	Sugars 19g	
Calories 113 Calories from Fat 9	Sodium 440mg	18%	Protein 4g	

Vitamin A 10% • Vitamin C 60% • Calcium 2% • Iron 6%
*Percent Daily Values (DV) are based on a 2000 calorie diet.

Menu Planning Guide
One serving of this recipe provides:
1 Fruit

Diet Exchanges:
½ starch • 1 fruit

Spicy Pumpkin Soup

Serve with roast turkey and a crusty dinner roll,
or Chicken Pasta Salad (p 75)

2   teaspoons olive oil
2   medium carrots, chopped (1 cup)
1   small onion, chopped (1/2 cup)
1   stalk celery, chopped (1/2 cup)
1/4   cup water
2   tablespoons packed brown sugar
2   teaspoons ground coriander
1   teaspoon ground cumin
1/2   teaspoon ground allspice
2 1/2   cups ready-to-serve chicken broth
1   can (16 oz.) pumpkin
1   medium russet potato, peeled and cut into
     1/2-inch cubes (1 cup)
     Plain nonfat or low-fat yogurt (optional)
     Toasted pumpkin seeds* (optional)

6 servings

*To toast pumpkin seeds, spread them on a baking
sheet, and bake at 325°F for 15 to 20 minutes, or
until golden brown, stirring occasionally.*

1 Heat oil over medium heat in 4-quart saucepan. Add carrots, onion, celery and water. Cook for 6 to 8 minutes, or until vegetables are tender, stirring occasionally.

2 Stir in sugar, coriander, cumin and allspice. Cook for 2 minutes, stirring constantly. Stir in broth, pumpkin and potato. Bring to boil. Reduce heat to low. Cover. Simmer for 20 minutes to blend flavors.

3 Place soup in food processor or blender. Process until smooth. Return soup to saucepan. Bring just to a simmer over medium-low heat, stirring frequently. Garnish each serving with dollop of yogurt and sprinkle with pumpkin seeds.

Nutrition Facts	Amount/serving	%DV*	Amount/serving	%DV*
Serving Size 1 cup (270g)	Total Fat 3g	4%	Total Carbohydrate 21g	7%
Servings per Recipe 6	Saturated Fat <1g	2%	Dietary Fiber 3g	13%
Calories 117	Cholesterol 0mg	0%	Sugars 7g	
Calories from Fat 23	Sodium 357mg	15%	Protein 4g	

Vitamin A 450% • Vitamin C 10% • Calcium 6% • Iron 10%
*Percent Daily Values (DV) are based on a 2000 calorie diet.

Menu Planning Guide
One serving of this recipe provides:
2 Vegetable

Diet Exchanges:
1 starch • 1 vegetable

Winter Squash & Leek Soup

Serve with Fisherman's Wharf Sandwiches (p 93) or Curried Chicken Salad Sandwiches (p 99)

1 butternut squash (2½ lbs.), peeled, seeded and cut into 2-inch chunks (6 to 7 cups)

3 cups water

2 medium leeks, thinly sliced (3 cups)

2 stalks celery, thinly sliced (1 cup)

½ cup ready-to-serve chicken broth

½ teaspoon ground nutmeg

½ teaspoon salt

¼ to ½ teaspoon freshly ground pepper

1 cup skim milk

Shredded fresh Parmesan cheese (optional)

8 servings

1 Combine squash and water in 4-quart saucepan. Bring to boil over high heat. Reduce heat to low. Simmer for 25 to 30 minutes, or until squash is very tender. Remove from heat. Cover to keep warm. Set aside.

2 Combine leeks, celery and broth in 6-quart Dutch oven or stockpot. Cook over low heat for 12 to 15 minutes, or until vegetables are tender, stirring occasionally. (Add additional chicken broth as needed to prevent vegetables from burning.)

3 Stir in squash mixture, nutmeg, salt and pepper. Cook over medium heat for 10 minutes. Blend in milk. Cook just until mixture begins to simmer. Remove from heat.

4 Place mixture in food processor or blender. Process until smooth. (You will have to process mixture in batches.) Serve immediately. Garnish individual servings with Parmesan cheese.

Nutrition Facts	Amount/serving	%DV*	Amount/serving	%DV*
Serving Size approximately 1 cup (359g) Servings per Recipe 8	Total Fat <1g	1%	Total Carbohydrate 22g	7%
	Saturated Fat 0g	0%	Dietary Fiber 6g	25%
	Cholesterol 0mg	0%	Sugars 9g	
Calories 95 Calories from Fat 4	Sodium 223mg	9%	Protein 4g	
	Vitamin A 110% • Vitamin C 15% • Calcium 10% • Iron 8%			
	*Percent Daily Values (DV) are based on a 2000 calorie diet.			

Menu Planning Guide

One serving of this recipe provides:

2 Vegetable

Diet Exchanges:

1 starch • 1 vegetable

Roasted Yellow Pepper Soup

Serve with Light Cobb Salad (p 80) or
Chicken Pasta Salad (p 75)

4 *medium yellow peppers*

1 *medium red pepper*

2 *teaspoons olive oil*

3/4 *cup finely chopped shallots*

1 *medium carrot, finely chopped (1/2 cup)*

3 *cups water*

1 *lb. red potatoes, peeled and cut into 1/2-inch cubes (about 2 1/2 cups)*

1 *teaspoon salt*

1/2 *teaspoon freshly ground pepper*

6 servings

Tip: Soup can be served chilled.

1 Place yellow and red peppers on baking sheet. Place under broiler with surface of peppers 1 to 2 inches from heat. Broil for 11 to 15 minutes, or until peppers blister and blacken, turning peppers frequently. Place yellow peppers in paper or plastic bag. Place red pepper in second paper or plastic bag. Seal bags. Let stand for 10 minutes.

2 Meanwhile, heat oil in 3-quart saucepan over medium heat. Add shallots and carrot. Cook for 2 1/2 to 3 minutes, or until carrot is tender-crisp, stirring frequently. Add water and potatoes. Bring to boil over high heat. Cover. Reduce heat to low. Simmer for 10 to 15 minutes, or until vegetables are very tender. Remove from heat. Set aside.

3 Peel, seed and coarsely chop all peppers. Set yellow peppers aside. In blender, process red pepper until smooth. Transfer to small bowl. Set aside.

4 Wash out blender. In blender, combine yellow peppers and potato mixture. Process until soup is smooth. (You will have to process soup in batches.)

5 Return soup to saucepan. Stir in salt and ground pepper. Cook over medium-low heat just until soup begins to simmer, stirring frequently. To serve, spoon about 1 cup soup into each serving bowl. Spoon processed red pepper in small dollops evenly over soup. Draw wooden pick or knife through red pepper to create a "feathered" look. (If desired, drizzle processed red pepper over soup in a zigzag pattern.)

Nutrition Facts	Amount/serving	%DV*	Amount/serving	%DV*
Serving Size approximately 1 cup (337g) Servings per Recipe 6 Calories 121 Calories from Fat 17	Total Fat 2g	3%	Total Carbohydrate 25g	8%
	Saturated Fat <1g	1%	Dietary Fiber 4g	16%
	Cholesterol 0mg	0%	Sugars 5g	
	Sodium 375mg	16%	Protein 3g	
	Vitamin A 90% • Vitamin C 370% • Calcium 4% • Iron 6%			
	*Percent Daily Values (DV) are based on a 2000 calorie diet.			

Menu Planning Guide
One serving of this recipe provides:
2 1/2 Vegetable

Diet Exchanges:
1 starch • 1 1/2 vegetable

Borscht

Serve with Egg Salad Sandwiches (p 87)
or Dilled Chicken Salad Sandwiches (p 103)

2 medium carrots, thinly sliced (1 cup)

1 medium onion, chopped (1 cup)

4½ cups hot water, divided

1 clove garlic, minced

1 can (16 oz.) julienne beets, rinsed and
   drained

1 cup shredded green cabbage

¼ cup red wine vinegar

2 tablespoons packed brown sugar

1 tablespoon plus 1 teaspoon very-low-sodium
   instant beef bouillon granules

½ to 1 teaspoon dried dill weed

⅛ teaspoon freshly ground pepper

6 servings

1 Combine carrots, onion, ½ cup water and the garlic in 3-quart saucepan. Cover. Cook over high heat for 5 to 6 minutes, or until vegetables are tender. Stir in remaining 4 cups water and remaining ingredients. Bring to boil. Reduce heat to low. Simmer for 6 to 10 minutes, or until cabbage is tender, stirring occasionally. Serve borscht with dollop of low-fat sour cream, if desired.

Nutrition Facts	Amount/serving	%DV*	Amount/serving	%DV*
Serving Size approximately 1 cup (308g)	Total Fat 1g	1%	Total Carbohydrate 13g	4%
	Saturated Fat 0g	0%	Dietary Fiber 3g	12%
Servings per Recipe 6	Cholesterol 0mg	0%	Sugars 8g	
Calories 59 Calories from Fat 5	Sodium 216mg	9%	Protein 2g	
	Vitamin A 110% • Vitamin C 10% • Calcium 4% • Iron 8%			
	*Percent Daily Values (DV) are based on a 2000 calorie diet.			

Menu Planning Guide

One serving of this recipe provides:

2 Vegetable

Diet Exchanges:

2 vegetable

Chicken Pasta Salad

*Serve with Spicy Pumpkin Soup (p 67) or
Roasted Yellow Pepper Soup (p 71)*

7 oz. uncooked small pasta shells

Dressing:

1/4 cup red wine vinegar

1/4 cup plain nonfat or low-fat yogurt

1/4 cup reduced-fat or nonfat mayonnaise

1/2 teaspoon dried tarragon leaves

1/4 teaspoon salt

1/4 teaspoon pepper

1 1/2 cups cubed cooked chicken breast (no skin;
        1/2-inch cubes)

1/2 cup frozen peas, defrosted and drained

1/2 cup chopped tomato

1/2 cup zucchini strips (2 x 1/8-inch strips)

1/4 cup finely chopped red onion

2 tablespoons snipped fresh parsley

6 servings

1 Prepare pasta as directed on package.
Rinse and drain. Set aside. In small mixing bowl, combine dressing ingredients.

2 Combine dressing, pasta and remaining
ingredients, except parsley, in large mixing bowl or salad bowl. Toss to combine.
Cover with plastic wrap. Chill. Garnish
salad with parsley.

Nutrition Facts	Amount/serving	%DV*	Amount/serving	%DV*
Serving Size approximately 1¼ cups (202g)	Total Fat 4g	6%	Total Carbohydrate 31g	10%
	Saturated Fat 1g	4%	Dietary Fiber 2g	9%
Servings per Recipe 6	Cholesterol 30mg	10%	Sugars 5g	
Calories 227 Calories from Fat 34	Sodium 194mg	8%	Protein 16g	

Vitamin A 6% • Vitamin C 15% • Calcium 4% • Iron 10%

*Percent Daily Values (DV) are based on a 2000 calorie diet.

Menu Planning Guide

One serving of this recipe provides:

1/2 Meat, Poultry & Fish
1/2 Vegetable
1 1/2 Bread, Cereal, Rice & Pasta

Diet Exchanges:

1 lean meat • 2 starch

Fruited Couscous Salad

Serve with Sweet & Sour Pineapple Soup (p 65)
or Ethiopian Lentil Stew (p 51)

1½ cups hot water
¼ teaspoon salt
1 cup uncooked couscous*
½ cup frozen orange juice concentrate,
    defrosted
2 tablespoons white wine vinegar
1 tablespoon sugar
1 tablespoon vegetable oil
1 teaspoon grated orange peel
1 cup fresh blueberries
1 cup fresh raspberries
1 cup fresh strawberries, hulled and cut in half
1 fresh peach, pitted and cut into ½-inch
    chunks
1 fresh plum, pitted and cut into ½-inch
    chunks
¼ cup fresh mint leaves

12 servings

*Couscous is a Middle-Eastern pasta available
in specialty markets and most supermarkets.*

1 Combine water and salt in 2-quart saucepan. Bring to boil over medium-high heat. Stir in couscous. Cover. Remove from heat. Let stand for 5 minutes. Fluff couscous lightly with fork. Place in medium mixing bowl. Set aside.

2 Combine concentrate, vinegar, sugar, oil and peel in 2-cup measure. Blend well with whisk. Add half of juice mixture to couscous. Mix well. Cover and chill at least 1 hour.

3 Add remaining juice mixture and remaining ingredients to couscous mixture. Toss gently to combine. Line serving bowl with lettuce, if desired.

Nutrition Facts	Amount/serving	%DV*	Amount/serving	%DV*	Menu Planning Guide
Serving Size 1 cup (123g)	Total Fat 2g	2%	Total Carbohydrate 25g	8%	One serving of this recipe provides:
Servings per Recipe 12	Saturated Fat <1g	1%	Dietary Fiber 3g	10%	½ Fruit
Calories 122	Cholesterol 0mg	0%	Sugars 9g		1 Bread, Cereal, Rice & Pasta
Calories from Fat 14	Sodium 4mg	0%	Protein 3g		
	Vitamin A 2% • Vitamin C 50% • Calcium 2% • Iron 2%				Diet Exchanges:
	*Percent Daily Values (DV) are based on a 2000 calorie diet.				1½ starch • ½ fruit

Warm New Potato Salad

Serve with Mushroom Soup (p 62)

1 lb. new potatoes, cut into quarters (3 cups)
3/4 cup water
2 cups frozen broccoli, green beans, pearl
    onions and red pepper vegetable mixture
1/3 cup plain nonfat or low-fat yogurt
1 tablespoon snipped fresh Italian parsley
    or cilantro leaves
1 tablespoon Dijon mustard
1/8 teaspoon salt

6 servings

1 Combine potatoes and water in 2-quart saucepan. Bring to boil over high heat. Cover. Reduce heat to low. Simmer for 15 to 20 minutes, or until potatoes are tender-crisp.

2 Stir in vegetable mixture. Re-cover. Increase heat to medium-high. Cook for 4 to 5 minutes, or until potatoes are tender and vegetables are hot, stirring occasionally. Drain. Set aside.

3 Combine remaining ingredients in serving bowl. Add potato mixture. Toss gently to coat. Serve warm.

Microwave tip: Decrease water to 2 tablespoons. In 2-quart casserole, combine potatoes and water. Cover. Microwave at High for 6 to 11 minutes, or until potatoes are tender-crisp, stirring once. Stir in vegetable mixture. Re-cover. Microwave at High for 4 to 7 minutes, or until potatoes are tender and vegetables are hot, stirring once or twice. Continue as directed.

Nutrition Facts	Amount/serving	%DV*	Amount/serving	%DV*	Menu Planning Guide
Serving Size approximately 1/2 cup (164g)	Total Fat <1g	0%	Total Carbohydrate 18g	6%	One serving of this recipe provides:
Servings per Recipe 6	Saturated Fat <1g	0%	Dietary Fiber 3g	10%	1 Vegetable
Calories 85	Cholesterol <1mg	0%	Sugars 3g		
Calories from Fat 3	Sodium 113mg	5%	Protein 3g		

Vitamin A 6% • Vitamin C 40% • Calcium 6% • Iron 4%
*Percent Daily Values (DV) are based on a 2000 calorie diet.

Diet Exchanges:
1 starch • 1/2 vegetable

Light Cobb Salad

*Serve with Split Pea Soup (p 44), Roasted Yellow Pepper Soup (p 71)
or Sweet Potato-Tomato Soup (p 60)*

8 *cups mixed salad greens*
2 *tablespoons fat-free blue cheese dressing
    or honey Dijon dressing*
½ *cup shredded cooked chicken breast (no skin)*
½ *cup halved cherry tomatoes*
½ *cup red and green pepper strips
    (2 x ¼-inch strips)*

½ *cup sliced fresh mushrooms*
⅓ *cup shredded carrot*
¼ *cup sliced green onions (1-inch slices)*
1 *hard-cooked egg, sliced*
⅛ *teaspoon paprika (optional)*
    Shredded fresh Parmesan cheese (optional)

2 servings

1 Combine salad greens and dressing in large mixing bowl. Toss to coat. Arrange salad evenly on two serving plates or in salad bowls.

2 Arrange remaining ingredients, except paprika and cheese, evenly in separate groups on top of salads. Sprinkle paprika over chicken. Sprinkle cheese evenly over salads. Serve immediately. Serve with additional fat-free dressing, if desired.

Nutrition Facts	Amount/serving	%DV*	Amount/serving	%DV*
Serving Size approximately 2½ cups (404g)	Total Fat 4g	6%	Total Carbohydrate 19g	6%
	Saturated Fat 1g	6%	Dietary Fiber 6g	24%
Servings per Recipe 2	Cholesterol 115mg	38%	Sugars 6g	
	Sodium 240mg	10%	Protein 16g	
Calories 166 Calories from Fat 37	Vitamin A 250% • Vitamin C 140% • Calcium 15% • Iron 25%			
	*Percent Daily Values (DV) are based on a 2000 calorie diet.			

Menu Planning Guide
One serving of this recipe provides:
1 Meat, Poultry & Fish
6 Vegetable

Diet Exchanges:
1½ lean meat • 3 vegetable

Crab & Shallot Salad

Serve with Hearty Vegetable-Barley Soup (p 58)

Salad:

- 4 cups torn fresh leaf lettuce
- 4 cups torn fresh spinach leaves
- 6 oz. shredded imitation crab legs
- ½ cup quartered red pearl onions
- ¼ cup finely chopped shallots
- ¼ cup shredded carrot
- 1 jalapeño pepper, seeded and finely chopped (optional)

Dressing:

- ¼ cup water
- 1 teaspoon unflavored gelatin
- 1 tablespoon sugar
- ½ teaspoon grated fresh lemon peel
- ¼ cup fresh lemon juice
- ½ teaspoon prepared yellow mustard
- ⅛ teaspoon pepper
  Dash paprika

6 servings

1 Combine salad ingredients in large mixing bowl or salad bowl. Cover with plastic wrap. Chill.

2 Place water in 1-quart saucepan. Sprinkle gelatin over water. Let stand for 1 minute to soften gelatin. Cook over low heat until gelatin is dissolved, stirring constantly. Remove from heat. Add sugar. Stir until dissolved.

3 Whisk in remaining dressing ingredients. Cool to room temperature, stirring occasionally. Pour dressing over salad. Toss gently to coat. Serve immediately.

Nutrition Facts	Amount/serving	%DV*	Amount/serving	%DV*
Serving Size approximately 1½ cups (151g)	Total Fat 1g	1%	Total Carbohydrate 11g	4%
	Saturated Fat 0g	0%	Dietary Fiber 2g	8%
Servings per Recipe 6	Cholesterol 6mg	2%	Sugars 6g	
Calories 69 Calories from Fat 6	Sodium 281mg	12%	Protein 6g	
	Vitamin A 90% • Vitamin C 40% • Calcium 8% • Iron 10%			
	*Percent Daily Values (DV) are based on a 2000 calorie diet.			

Menu Planning Guide

One serving of this recipe provides:

1½ Vegetable

Diet Exchanges:

½ meat • ½ starch

Spinach & Shallot Dressing

Serve over sliced tomato salad with Italian Vegetable Soup (p 55)

6 cups coarsely torn fresh spinach leaves,
   divided

¼ cup finely chopped shallots

¼ cup apple jelly

2 tablespoons white wine vinegar

¼ teaspoon dried tarragon leaves

⅛ teaspoon salt

   Mixed salad greens, torn into bite-size
   pieces (optional)

   Tomato slices (optional)

12 servings

1 Combine 1 cup spinach, the shallots, jelly, vinegar, tarragon and salt in food processor or blender. Process until smooth. Add remaining 5 cups spinach, 1 cup at a time, processing after each addition until dressing is smooth.

2 Arrange greens and tomato slices on serving dishes. Spoon 2 tablespoons dressing over each serving. Refrigerate remaining dressing up to 1 week in airtight container.

Nutrition Facts	Amount/serving	%DV*	Amount/serving	%DV*
Serving Size 2 tablespoons (40g)	Total Fat <1g	0%	Total Carbohydrate 6g	2%
	Saturated Fat <1g	0%	Dietary Fiber 1g	4%
Servings per Recipe 12	Cholesterol 0mg	0%	Sugars 5g	
Calories 25 Calories from Fat 1	Sodium 47mg	2%	Protein 1g	
	Vitamin A 45% • Vitamin C 15% • Calcium 2% • Iron 4%			
	*Percent Daily Values (DV) are based on a 2000 calorie diet.			

Menu Planning Guide

One serving of this recipe provides:

½ Vegetable

Diet Exchanges:

½ vegetable

Egg Salad Sandwiches

Serve with Borscht (p 72) or Potato-Leek Soup (p 56)

4 hard-cooked eggs
1 tablespoon plain nonfat or low-fat yogurt
1 tablespoon reduced-fat or nonfat mayonnaise
1 teaspoon spicy brown mustard
2 tablespoons finely chopped green onion
2 tablespoons finely chopped celery
1/8 teaspoon salt
1/8 teaspoon pepper
4 slices pumpernickel bread

4 servings

1 Separate egg yolks and whites. Reserve 3 yolks for future use. In small mixing bowl, mash remaining egg yolk with fork. Add yogurt, mayonnaise and mustard. Mix well.

2 Chop egg whites. Add egg whites, onion, celery, salt and pepper to egg yolk mixture. Stir gently to combine. Chill. Spread mixture evenly on bread slices.

Nutrition Facts	Amount/serving	%DV*	Amount/serving	%DV*
Serving Size 1 sandwich (86g)	Total Fat 3g	5%	Total Carbohydrate 17g	6%
	Saturated Fat 1g	3%	Dietary Fiber 2g	8%
Servings per Recipe 4	Cholesterol 55mg	18%	Sugars 3g	
Calories 126 Calories from Fat 27	Sodium 380mg	16%	Protein 7g	
	Vitamin A 2% • Vitamin C 2% • Calcium 4% • Iron 6%			
	*Percent Daily Values (DV) are based on a 2000 calorie diet.			

Menu Planning Guide
One serving of this recipe provides:
1/2 Meat, Poultry & Fish
1 Bread, Cereal, Rice & Pasta

Diet Exchanges:
1 lean meat • 1 starch

Barbecued Chicken Sandwich

Serve with Split Pea Soup (p 44)

1 boneless whole chicken breast (8 to 10 oz.),
  cut in half, skin removed

1 small onion, sliced (½ cup)

¼ cup chopped green pepper

1 clove garlic, minced

1 teaspoon olive oil

1 can (8 oz.) no-salt-added tomato sauce

3 tablespoons tomato paste

2 tablespoons packed brown sugar

1 tablespoon red wine vinegar

1 tablespoon Worcestershire sauce

½ teaspoon dry mustard

4 drops red pepper sauce

4 whole wheat hamburger buns

4 servings

1 Heat oven to 350°F. Place chicken breast in 8-inch square baking dish. Cover with foil. Bake for 20 to 25 minutes, or until meat is no longer pink and juices run clear. Set aside.

2 Place onion, green pepper, garlic and oil in 10-inch nonstick skillet. Cook over medium heat for 3 to 5 minutes, or until vegetables are tender, stirring frequently. Add remaining ingredients, except chicken and buns. Cook over medium heat for 5 minutes, or until barbecue sauce is slightly thickened and flavors are blended, stirring frequently.

3 Shred chicken. Add to barbecue sauce. Cover. Cook over medium heat for 4 to 5 minutes, or until hot, stirring occasionally. Spoon ½ cup mixture onto each bun.

Microwave tip: Place chicken breast on roasting rack or in 8-inch square baking dish. Cover with wax paper. Microwave at High for 4 to 6 minutes, or until meat is no longer pink and juices run clear, rotating once. Continue as directed.

Nutrition Facts	Amount/serving	%DV*	Amount/serving	%DV*
Serving Size 1 sandwich (199g)	Total Fat 7g	10%	Total Carbohydrate 37g	12%
Servings per Recipe 4	Saturated Fat 2g	8%	Dietary Fiber 3g	12%
Calories 269	Cholesterol 30mg	10%	Sugars 12g	
Calories from Fat 59	Sodium 435mg	18%	Protein 16g	

Vitamin A 20% • Vitamin C 35% • Calcium 10% • Iron 15%
*Percent Daily Values (DV) are based on a 2000 calorie diet.

Menu Planning Guide

One serving of this recipe provides:

½ Meat, Poultry & Fish
1 Vegetable
2 Bread, Cereal, Rice & Pasta

Diet Exchanges:

1 lean meat • 2 starch • 1 vegetable

South of the Border Muffuletta

Serve with Tortilla Soup (p 46) or Black Bean Chili (p 40)

1 loaf (1 lb.) round sourdough bread
¼ cup nonfat yogurt cheese*
1 tablespoon sliced green onion
1 clove garlic, minced
1 teaspoon Dijon mustard
⅛ teaspoon chili powder
⅛ teaspoon ground cumin
⅛ teaspoon ground turmeric
6 slices (0.5 oz. each) fully cooked chicken breast
3 slices (1 oz. each) reduced-fat Monterey
   Jack cheese

1 can (4 oz.) whole green chilies,
   drained and sliced in half lengthwise
4 slices tomato
   Leaf lettuce

8 servings

* Make yogurt cheese by spooning gelatin-free yogurt into paper-towel-lined strainer. Place over bowl and let drain overnight in refrigerator.

1 Cut loaf in half crosswise. Cut circle 1 inch from outer edge of crust. Remove bread from circle to 1-inch depth. Reserve bread for future use. Set halves aside.

2 Combine yogurt cheese, onion, garlic, mustard, chili powder, cumin and turmeric in small mixing bowl. Spread yogurt cheese mixture evenly over inside of top and bottom halves of loaf.

3 Layer 2 chicken slices, 1 cheese slice, half of chilies, 2 tomato slices and lettuce on bottom half of loaf. Repeat layers once. Top with 2 chicken slices and 1 cheese slice. Place top half of loaf over filling. Serve in wedges.

Nutrition Facts	Amount/serving	%DV*	Amount/serving	%DV*
Serving Size 1 wedge (113g)	Total Fat 4g	6%	Total Carbohydrate 32g	11%
Servings per Recipe 8	Saturated Fat 2g	8%	Dietary Fiber 2g	8%
Calories 217	Cholesterol 17mg	6%	Sugars 2g	
Calories from Fat 37	Sodium 464mg	19%	Protein 12g	

Vitamin A 6% • Vitamin C 8% • Calcium 15% • Iron 10%
*Percent Daily Values (DV) are based on a 2000 calorie diet.

Menu Planning Guide
One serving of this recipe provides:
2 Bread, Cereal, Rice & Pasta

Diet Exchanges:
1 lean meat • 2 starch

Fisherman's Wharf Sandwiches

Serve with Winter Squash & Leek Soup (p 68)

8 oz. frozen cooked cocktail shrimp*, defrosted and drained

1/3 cup shredded part-skim or nonfat mozzarella cheese

1/3 cup finely chopped red pepper

1/4 cup fat-free mayonnaise

2 tablespoons sliced green onion

2 teaspoons fresh lemon juice

1/4 teaspoon freshly ground pepper

3 whole wheat pita loaves (6-inch), cut in half; or 6 sourdough buns, split

Fresh alfalfa sprouts

1 Combine shrimp, cheese, red pepper, mayonnaise, onion, juice and pepper in medium mixing bowl. Spoon 1/3 cup mixture into each pita half. Top with sprouts.

6 servings

Shrimp may range in size from tiny to medium.

Nutrition Facts	Amount/serving	%DV*	Amount/serving	%DV*	Menu Planning Guide
Serving Size 1 sandwich (87g)	Total Fat 2g	3%	Total Carbohydrate 15g	5%	One serving of this recipe provides:
Servings per Recipe 6	Saturated Fat <1g	4%	Dietary Fiber 2g	8%	1/2 Meat, Poultry & Fish 1 Bread, Cereal, Rice & Pasta
Calories 125	Cholesterol 77mg	26%	Sugars 1g		
Calories from Fat 18	Sodium 350mg	15%	Protein 12g		

Vitamin A 8% • Vitamin C 20% • Calcium 6% • Iron 10%
*Percent Daily Values (DV) are based on a 2000 calorie diet.

Diet Exchanges:
1 lean meat • 1 starch

Hearty Tuna Sandwiches

Serve with Sweet & Sour Pineapple Soup (p 65) or Italian Vegetable Soup (p 55)

1 can (6¹⁄8 oz.) no-salt-added tuna, rinsed and drained

1 stalk celery, chopped (¹⁄2 cup)

¹⁄4 cup fat-free Italian dressing

1 tablespoon chopped black olives (optional)

¹⁄4 teaspoon dried thyme leaves

2 teaspoons Dijon or prepared mustard

4 slices rye bread, toasted

4 slices (³⁄4 oz. each) low-fat pasteurized process American cheese singles (optional)

8 slices tomato

4 servings

1 Combine tuna, celery, dressing, olives and thyme in small mixing bowl. Set aside. Spread mustard evenly on toast. Place 1 slice cheese on each slice toast. Spread heaping ¹⁄3 cup tuna mixture over each slice cheese. Top each sandwich with 2 slices tomato.

Nutrition Facts	Amount/serving	%DV*	Amount/serving	%DV*
Serving Size 1 sandwich (130g)	Total Fat 1g	2%	Total Carbohydrate 16g	5%
	Saturated Fat <1g	1%	Dietary Fiber 2g	8%
Servings per Recipe 4	Cholesterol 7mg	2%	Sugars 3g	
Calories 133 Calories from Fat 12	Sodium 481mg	20%	Protein 14g	
	Vitamin A 6% • Vitamin C 15% • Calcium 4% • Iron 15%			
	*Percent Daily Values (DV) are based on a 2000 calorie diet.			

Menu Planning Guide

One serving of this recipe provides:

½ Meat, Poultry & Fish
1 Bread, Cereal, Rice & Pasta

Diet Exchanges:

1½ lean meat • 1 starch

Meatball Hoagies

Serve with Sweet Potato-Tomato Soup (p 60)

½ lb. ground chicken (breast meat only; no skin), crumbled

1 cup uncooked instant white rice

2 cans (8 oz. each) no-salt-added tomato sauce, divided

¼ cup frozen cholesterol-free egg product, defrosted; or 1 egg, beaten

¼ cup finely chopped onion

1 tablespoon dried parsley flakes

½ teaspoon pepper, divided

1 tablespoon tomato paste

½ teaspoon dry mustard

½ teaspoon dried oregano leaves

¼ teaspoon dried basil leaves

1 fresh baguette (8 oz.), 20 inches long

4 servings

1 Combine chicken, rice, ¼ cup tomato sauce, the egg product, onion, parsley and ¼ teaspoon pepper in medium mixing bowl. Shape into 12 meatballs. Place in 10-inch nonstick skillet. In 2-cup measure, combine remaining tomato sauce, the tomato paste, mustard, oregano, basil and remaining ¼ teaspoon pepper.

2 Pour sauce over meatballs. Bring sauce to boil over high heat. Cover. Reduce heat to medium. Simmer for 10 to 12 minutes, or until meatballs are firm and no longer pink, carefully turning meatballs over occasionally. Remove from heat. Cover to keep warm. Set aside.

3 Cut baguette crosswise into four 5-inch sections. Cut lengthwise piece out of each baguette section to within ½ inch of bottom and sides. Remove pieces. (If desired, trim pieces to ½-inch thickness.) Spoon meatballs and sauce evenly into baguette sections. Top meatballs with baguette pieces.

Nutrition Facts	Amount/serving	%DV*	Amount/serving	%DV*
Serving Size 1 hoagie (323g)	Total Fat 4g	6%	Total Carbohydrate 58g	19%
Servings per Recipe 4	Saturated Fat 1g	5%	Dietary Fiber 4g	16%
Calories 357	Cholesterol 35mg	12%	Sugars 6g	
Calories from Fat 34	Sodium 462mg	19%	Protein 23g	

Vitamin A 30% • Vitamin C 30% • Calcium 10% • Iron 25%
*Percent Daily Values (DV) are based on a 2000 calorie diet.

Menu Planning Guide
One serving of this recipe provides:
1 Meat, Poultry & Fish
1 Vegetable
3 Bread, Cereal, Rice & Pasta

Diet Exchanges:
1½ lean meat • 3½ starch • 1 vegetable

Curried Chicken Salad Sandwiches

Serve with Winter Squash & Leek Soup (p 68)

2 boneless whole chicken breasts (8 to 10 oz. each), split in half, skin removed

1¾ teaspoons curry powder, divided

1 small onion, chopped (½ cup)

2 cloves garlic, minced

1 teaspoon olive oil

½ cup low-fat sour cream

1 tablespoon grated fresh gingerroot

1 tablespoon snipped fresh cilantro

2 teaspoons sugar

¼ teaspoon salt

⅛ teaspoon crushed red pepper flakes

¼ cup sliced celery

¼ cup shredded carrot

6 whole wheat pita halves or 6 warm popovers

6 servings

1 Heat oven to 350°F. Rub chicken with 1½ teaspoons curry powder. Place chicken in 8-inch square baking dish. Cover with foil. Bake for 25 to 30 minutes, or until meat is no longer pink and juices run clear. Drain. Cool slightly. Cut chicken into ¾-inch pieces. Cover to keep warm. Set aside.

2 Combine onion, garlic and oil in 8-inch nonstick skillet. Cook over medium heat for 4½ to 6½ minutes, or until onion is tender, stirring frequently. In food processor or blender, combine onion mixture, remaining ¼ teaspoon curry powder, the sour cream, gingerroot, cilantro, sugar, salt and pepper flakes. Process until almost smooth.

3 Combine processed onion mixture, chicken, celery and carrot in medium mixing bowl. Serve chicken salad warm in pita halves.

Microwave tip: Place chicken on roasting rack or in 8-inch square baking dish. Cover with wax paper. Microwave at High for 4 to 9 minutes, or until meat is no longer pink and juices run clear, rearranging once. Continue as directed.

Nutrition Facts	Amount/serving	%DV*	Amount/serving	%DV*
Serving Size ½ pita (119g)	Total Fat 6g	9%	Total Carbohydrate 18g	6%
	Saturated Fat 2g	11%	Dietary Fiber 2g	10%
Servings per Recipe 6	Cholesterol 48mg	16%	Sugars 4g	
Calories 190	Sodium 259mg	11%	Protein 18g	
Calories from Fat 50	Vitamin A 30% • Vitamin C 4% • Calcium 4% • Iron 8%			
	*Percent Daily Values (DV) are based on a 2000 calorie diet.			

Menu Planning Guide

One serving of this recipe provides:
1 Meat, Poultry & Fish
1 Bread, Cereal, Rice & Pasta

Diet Exchanges:

2 lean meat • 1 starch

Black Bean Tortilla Pockets

Serve with Tortilla Soup (p 46) or Tofu Chili (p 49)

1 can (15 oz.) black beans, rinsed and
   drained

½ cup chopped seeded tomato

¼ cup chopped cucumber

¼ cup plain nonfat or low-fat yogurt

1 clove garlic, minced

¼ to ½ teaspoon dried dill weed

¼ teaspoon pepper

4 flour tortillas (8-inch)

¼ cup alfalfa sprouts

4 servings

1 Combine beans, tomato, cucumber, yogurt, garlic, dill weed and pepper in medium mixing bowl. Spoon ½ cup bean mixture into center of each tortilla. Top evenly with sprouts. Fold sides of tortillas in. Bring bottoms of tortillas up. Secure with wooden picks.

Nutrition Facts	Amount/serving	%DV*	Amount/serving	%DV*
Serving Size 1 pocket (175g)	Total Fat 4g	5%	Total Carbohydrate 38g	13%
Servings per Recipe 4	Saturated Fat <1g	2%	Dietary Fiber 7g	27%
Calories 205	Cholesterol 0mg	0%	Sugars 2g	
Calories from Fat 32	Sodium 469mg	20%	Protein 12g	

Vitamin A 4% • Vitamin C 8% • Calcium 10% • Iron 15%
*Percent Daily Values (DV) are based on a 2000 calorie diet.

Menu Planning Guide
One serving of this recipe provides:
½ Meat, Poultry & Fish
1 Bread, Cereal, Rice & Pasta

Diet Exchanges:
2½ starch

Dilled Chicken Salad Sandwiches

Serve with Borscht (p 72)

¼ cup frozen baby peas

½ cup plain nonfat or low-fat yogurt

2 teaspoons prepared yellow mustard

1 teaspoon snipped fresh dill weed

1 teaspoon sugar

½ teaspoon grated lemon peel

¼ teaspoon white pepper

⅛ teaspoon garlic powder

2 cups chilled shredded cooked chicken breast

¼ cup finely chopped celery

¼ cup finely chopped shallots

8 slices whole wheat bread, toasted

8 slices tomato

   Lettuce leaves

4 servings

Tip: Add ¼ cup chopped cashews to chicken salad, if desired.

1 Line 8-inch square baking pan with paper towel. Spread peas evenly in prepared pan. Defrost completely. Set aside.

2 Combine yogurt, mustard, dill, sugar, peel, pepper and garlic powder in medium mixing bowl. Stir in peas, chicken, celery and shallots. Place lettuce on half of toast slices. Spread evenly with chicken salad. Top with tomato slices and remaining slices of toast.

Nutrition Facts	Amount/serving	%DV*	Amount/serving	%DV*
Serving Size 1 sandwich (239g) Servings per Recipe 4 Calories 339 Calories from Fat 76	Total Fat 8g	13%	Total Carbohydrate 39g	13%
	Saturated Fat 2g	11%	Dietary Fiber 6g	25%
	Cholesterol 53mg	18%	Sugars 8g	
	Sodium 465mg	19%	Protein 29g	

Vitamin A 35% • Vitamin C 20% • Calcium 15% • Iron 20%

*Percent Daily Values (DV) are based on a 2000 calorie diet.

Menu Planning Guide
One serving of this recipe provides:
1 Meat, Poultry & Fish
1 Vegetable
2 Bread, Cereal, Rice & Pasta

Diet Exchanges:
2½ lean meat • 2 starch • 1 vegetable

Mediterranean Tuna Sandwich

Serve with Mushroom Soup (p 62)

1 loaf (12 oz.) round hearty whole-grain bread

Vinaigrette:

¼ cup plain nonfat or low-fat yogurt

3 tablespoons red wine vinegar

1 tablespoon olive oil

1 tablespoon snipped fresh Italian parsley

1 teaspoon Dijon mustard

1 clove garlic, minced

2 cups coarsely torn fresh romaine leaves

1 can (6 oz.) water-pack chunk white tuna, rinsed and drained

1 small cucumber, thinly sliced (1 cup)

1 medium tomato, thinly sliced

½ medium red pepper, thinly sliced

½ medium green pepper, thinly sliced

½ small red onion, thinly sliced

6 servings

Tip: This sandwich is good for making ahead and packing for a lunch or picnic.

1 Cut loaf in half crosswise. Cut circle 1 inch from outer edge of crust. Remove bread from circle to 1-inch depth. Coarsely tear bread. (Toast, if desired.) Reserve bread. Set halves aside.

2 Combine vinaigrette ingredients in small mixing bowl. Whisk until smooth. In large mixing bowl, combine vinaigrette, reserved bread, the romaine and tuna.

3 Fill bottom half of loaf with tuna mixture. Layer remaining ingredients over tuna mixture. Place top half of loaf over filling. Wrap sandwich with plastic wrap. Chill 30 minutes. Cut into 6 wedges to serve.

Nutrition Facts	Amount/serving	%DV*	Amount/serving	%DV*
Serving Size 1 wedge (181g)	Total Fat 6g	8%	Total Carbohydrate 31g	10%
Servings per Recipe 6	Saturated Fat 1g	5%	Dietary Fiber 5g	20%
Calories 217	Cholesterol 10mg	4%	Sugars 5g	
Calories from Fat 50	Sodium 434mg	18%	Protein 14g	

Vitamin A 20% • Vitamin C 45% • Calcium 8% • Iron 15%
*Percent Daily Values (DV) are based on a 2000 calorie diet.

Menu Planning Guide

One serving of this recipe provides:

½ Meat, Poultry & Fish
1 Vegetable
2 Bread, Cereal, Rice & Pasta

Diet Exchanges:

1 lean meat • 2 starch • 1 vegetable

Denver Omelet Sandwiches

Serve with Mexican Corn Chowder (p 52)

1 cup frozen cholesterol-free egg product,
    defrosted; or 4 eggs, beaten

1/4 cup cubed low-fat fully cooked ham
    (1/4-inch cubes)

1/4 cup finely chopped green pepper

1/4 cup finely chopped onion

1/8 teaspoon pepper
    Dash red pepper sauce

4 bagels, split in half and toasted; or 8 slices
    whole wheat bread, toasted

4 slices (3/4 oz. each) fat-free pasteurized
    process cheese product (optional)

4 slices tomato
    Lettuce leaves

4 servings

*Tip: If desired, omit tomato slices. Serve sand-
wich with prepared salsa.*

1 Combine egg product, ham, green pepper, onion, pepper and red pepper sauce in small mixing bowl. Set aside. Spray 7-inch nonstick skillet with nonstick vegetable cooking spray. Heat skillet over medium-low heat. Pour 1/3 cup egg product mixture into skillet, tilting skillet to coat bottom. Cook for 3 1/2 to 6 minutes, or until omelet is set and bottom is lightly browned. Remove from heat.

2 Fold omelet in half, then in half again. Place omelet on 1 bagel half. Place 1 slice cheese, 1 slice tomato and lettuce over omelet. Top with remaining bagel half. Repeat with remaining egg product mixture, bagels, cheese, tomato slices and lettuce. Serve immediately.

Nutrition Facts	Amount/serving	%DV*	Amount/serving	%DV*	Menu Planning Guide
Serving Size 1 sandwich (190g)	Total Fat 2g	2%	Total Carbohydrate 40g	13%	One serving of this recipe provides:
	Saturated Fat <1g	1%	Dietary Fiber 2g	9%	1/2 Meat, Poultry & Fish
Servings per Recipe 4	Cholesterol 4mg	1%	Sugars 3g		2 Bread, Cereal, Rice & Pasta
Calories 235	Sodium 539mg	22%	Protein 16g		
Calories from Fat 14	Vitamin A 15% • Vitamin C 20% • Calcium 8% • Iron 20%				
	*Percent Daily Values (DV) are based on a 2000 calorie diet.				

Diet Exchanges:
1 lean meat • 2 1/2 starch

TLT's with Herbed Mayonnaise

Serve with Potato-Leek Soup (p 56)

¼ cup nonfat or reduced-fat mayonnaise

⅛ to ¼ teaspoon dried thyme leaves

⅛ teaspoon pepper

2 tablespoons fresh lime juice

⅛ teaspoon dried marjoram leaves

1 lb. uncooked turkey breast slices (¼ inch thick), cut into 1-inch strips

8 slices whole wheat bread, toasted
  Leaf lettuce

8 to 12 slices tomato

4 servings

1 Combine mayonnaise, thyme and pepper in small bowl. Cover with plastic wrap. Chill. In shallow dish, combine juice and marjoram. Add turkey strips, stirring to coat.

2 Spray 12-inch nonstick skillet with nonstick vegetable cooking spray. Heat skillet over medium-high heat. Add half of turkey strips. Cook for 6 to 8 minutes, or until meat is no longer pink and strips are browned on both sides, turning strips over once. Remove strips from skillet. Cover to keep warm. Repeat with remaining turkey strips.

3 Spread mayonnaise mixture evenly over 4 toast slices. Top evenly with lettuce, tomato slices and turkey strips. Top with remaining toast slices. Serve immediately.

Nutrition Facts	Amount/serving	%DV*	Amount/serving	%DV*
Serving Size 1 sandwich (222g)	Total Fat 4g	5%	Total Carbohydrate 33g	11%
Servings per Recipe 4	Saturated Fat 1g	4%	Dietary Fiber 4g	16%
Calories 289	Cholesterol 72mg	24%	Sugars 4g	
Calories from Fat 32	Sodium 522mg	22%	Protein 31g	
	Vitamin A 6% • Vitamin C 20% • Calcium 8% • Iron 20%			
	*Percent Daily Values (DV) are based on a 2000 calorie diet.			

Menu Planning Guide
One serving of this recipe provides:
1 Meat, Poultry & Fish
2 Bread, Cereal, Rice & Pasta

Diet Exchanges:
3 lean meat • 2 starch

Index

Cy DeCosse Incorporated offers
a variety of how-to books.
For information write:
    Cy DeCosse Subscriber Books
    5900 Green Oak Drive
    Minnetonka, MN 55343